P9-AOH-288

LORD PORTAL
H.M.S.T.C.
LORD PORTAL

Ballada
PUOLA
BALLADA

FINLAND

N·W·DAMM & SØN

Contents

Introduction

Looking down at Finland from a plane in the summertime, this country, which stretches some 1,160 kilometres from north to south and 540 kilometres from east to west, presents a blue-green expanse of forests and lakes. In the wintertime the same landscape is completely white. As the plane begins its descent signs of habitation start to appear among the trees, lakes and rivers. Towns and a few cities can be seen nestling in the vast open tracts of rural landscape.

Roughly one tenth of the total area of the country is covered by water. In fact Finland has 56,012 lakes with surface areas greater than 1,000m² and 187,888 lakes over 500 m² in area.

The country is situated between Sweden and Russia and borders Norway to the north. Finland's maritime borders with Sweden, Estonia and Russia extend over more than 1,100 kilometres.

Nuorgam, on the Finnish border with Norway, is the northernmost point of the European Union, the easternmost point being Lake Virmajärvi in Ilomantsi, close to Russia. Here you can obtain special permission to visit the border zone which lies just a stone's throw away from the Russian forests.

The Finnish archipelago is made up of beautiful islands of bare rock as well as islands covered with lush, green deciduous forests and flowering meadows. It is a unique winter experience to travel from Helsinki or Turku to Stockholm on one of the huge car ferries that plough through the ice-fields as easily as ice-breakers.

Although Finland is the fifth largest country in Europe in terms of area, it has a population of just 5.2 million. Six per cent of the inhabitants speak Swedish as their native language and Finland is officially a bilingual country. The Swedish-speaking Finns are on good terms with the Finnish-speaking majority and there has never been any animosity between the two groups.

The timber industry is extremely important to the Finnish economy, accounting for roughly one third of the country's export industry.

It is not without reason that Finland is known as the country of a thousand lakes. The water is pure enough to drink.

In the north of Finland the sun stays below the horizon from mid-December to mid-January, but the white snow and the rays of the hidden sun glowing from below the horizon turn the landscape into a fairy-tale scene.

Haypoles are the good fairies of the fields
In July haypoles can still be seen in many fields in Finland. They are exactly the same as they were hundreds of years ago, drying hay for cows, horses and other farm animals.
The dancer Reijo Kela was born in eastern Finland in Suomussalmi. Kela's provocative choreography often helps us see things in a new, deeper way.

The title of the work Kela has brought to the hayfields of his home province, Quiet Nation, could hardly be more appropriate. Each spring this multi-talented artist prepares his 'nation' for a new performance telling the story of the Finns – a people who are quiet, a little reserved and typically unwilling to be too ready with their opinions.

Stone Age Artists

There are over sixty known rock paintings in Finland, with the oldest dating back to the early Stone Age (about 3500 BC) and the most recent dating from the earliest centuries AD. Rock painting is a form of prehistoric art that is specific to Finland.

Elsewhere artwork of a similar kind took the form of drawing. The most common subjects of these early works of art are elks and people. The pictures were painted on sheer rock walls that plunge straight down into the water so that hunters travelling by boat could see them. Sacrifices were offered to the images both before and after hunting.

Near Ristiina in South Savo there lived a tribe of artist-hunters who painted the largest group of rock paintings in Scandinavia on the sheer cliffs of Astuvansalmi Strait. Measuring some fifteen metres from end to end, the paintings are a series of narrative images of elks, people and boats, as well as palm prints. Some of the human figures are wearing what appear to be antlers; these are thought to depict shamans dressed as elks. In the ancient religion of the Finno-Ugric peoples the boat symbolised the ship of the soul in which the deceased sailed to their final end after death. The prows of these boats were often adorned with carvings of elk heads.

The paintings at Astuvansalmi, which contain over 60 figures, were not discovered until 1968.

Rock paintings in South Karelia include the same motifs of elks, people and boats, but some of them also depict birds and snakes. The pictures on the rocks were painted by people in boats in the summer or standing on the ice in winter. The images are painted at different heights and this enables us to date changes in the shoreline and the rise and fall of the water level in the lakes. Looking at these pictures, you get a vivid impression of the culture of the ancestors of the Finns who survived by hunting elk, deer and bear.

Utensils and tools were adorned with the likenesses of the animals hunted by the people. Weapons were decorated with skilfully-wrought images of an elk or bear head, while wooden spoons were usually graced with the head of an elk. The elk is the most common figure found on utensils and tools as well as in the rock paintings. In a painting at Muuraisvuori Hill, Luumäki, eight men are depicted in a boat, the prow of which is adorned with the proud head of an elk.

The beautiful virgin forest in the hiking area of Hossa, in Kainuu, also has a well-preserved group of prehistoric rock paintings. Here, too, the most common motifs are men and elks. This far north the elks in the paintings have no antlers, indicating that elk hunting took place in the spring before the antlers had grown. Many of the elks have a red heart, the centre of life, painted on their breast. It was believed that this was a way of capturing the soul of the animal.

All the rock paintings were painted with red pigment which was considered a sacred colour and believed to provide protection against evil forces. This red pigment was made from a mixture of blood, grease and red earth. Red earth paint was thus already in use in prehistoric times. It was made by heating up ferrous material dug from the ground. For hundreds of years red earth has been the typical colour for painting wooden houses in Finland because it gives a durable and attractive finish. Some six thousand years ago Finns even buried their dead in graves of red earth to symbolise the hope that life continues after death.

The first discovery of a rock painting in Finland was made in 1911 on Lake Hvitträsk in Kirkkonummi, near Helsinki, by the man who is perhaps the most well-known Finn in the world, the great composer Jean Sibelius.

Sibelius and Finland

On 8 December 1865, in the small town of Hämeenlinna, a second child was born to Christian Sibelius, the town's doctor, and his wife Maria. Christened Johan Christian Julius, the boy was called Janne at home, but he later changed his name to Jean.

The objects in Sibelius' birthplace in Hämeenlinna reveal as much about the life of his family as about the spirit of the age.

Jean Sibelius was only two years old when his father died in the typhoid fever epidemic. Grief was soon followed by financial ruin. Jean's father had never been good at managing his finances and the family was forced to move into a house owned by Maria's mother. A third child was born after Jean's father had died.

Jean went to school in Hämeenlinna and played in the school orchestra from an early age. His older sister and younger brother were also musically gifted. Both their parents came from musical families. Jean's father, Christian, had played the guitar. He was regarded as a romantic, authentic, "divinely naive" and good-hearted man. Later in life Jean Sibelius said:
"... everything that is naive in me – however lacking in inner logic – means so much to my soul."

The Sibelius family home in Hämeenlinna is now a museum. The house was built in 1834 and was rented by the family until the death of Jean's father. It contains a piano, of course, which was also rented when the family lived there. There were also five bird cages in the house and the rooms were filled with pot plants. This cosy museum is a good place to begin learning about one of the world's most popular composers.

Near the town of Vaasa, on the western coast of Finland, stands the former Tottesund Manor with its main building which dates back to the 1800s. On 10 June 1892 it played host to a grand wedding. Aino, the youngest daughter of Alexander Järnefelt, the governor of Vaasa, was married to a promising young composer named Jean Sibelius. The newlyweds set out on their honeymoon by boat from the manor park, but a storm blew up and they had to continue their journey on foot. From Vaasa the couple travelled through Imatra to Lieksa and then on to the shores of Lake Pielinen. Pielinen is situated near Koli, a range of wooded hills which is an area of outstanding beauty in Finland. Koli has since been declared a national

Aino and Jean Sibelius both lived and died at Ainola, their house in Järvenpää, not far from Helsinki.
The house is now a museum. The maestro's favourite place was the easy chair in his study.

park. Formed from the remnants of a once great range of mountains, Koli proved a source of inspiration for many Finnish artists, including Jean Sibelius.

Aino Sibelius (1871–1969) came from an extraordinary family. Her father, Lieutenant General Alexander Järnefelt, was also a topographer and an accomplished administrator. Her mother, Elisabeth, was a powerful personality, a talented writer and one of the strongest women of her time. She had a love affair with Juhani Aho, the first Finnish professional writer, who was 22 years her junior.

Along with Jean Sibelius, Aino's three brothers – Armas, a conductor and composer, Arvid, a writer and fearless follower of the philosophy of Tolstoy, and Eero, one of the masters of the Golden Age of Finnish painting – were all significant figures in Finland's struggle for independence.

In the autumn of 1909 Jean Sibelius travelled to Koli with his brother-in-law, Eero Järnefelt. The magnificent vistas of Koli and Lake Pielisjärvi not only brought back fond memories of his honeymoon, but also gave him new strength. Sibelius wrote in his diary that visiting Koli was the greatest experience of his life. The pictures Eero Järnefelt painted during their trip to Koli are ranked among the most precious treasures of Finnish national art.

The trip to Koli resulted in Sibelius' Fourth Symphony which he began composing upon his return in April but did not complete until 1911. The work was interrupted by other assignments which Sibelius was forced to take on in order to pay his debts and manage his finances. In 1910 Sibelius made the following entry in his diary: "Money matters are to me like going to the toilet, a necessary evil."

Sibelius conducted the first performance of his Fourth Symphony in Helsinki in April 1911. Although the public and the critics did not quite grasp the piece, it was a revelation for other Finnish composers – like the Bible it was a repository of stories about the fathomless tragedy of the contradictions of life itself.

Today, tourists with an interest in the arts like to visit the area around Lake Tuusulanjärvi near Helsinki. Around the

The Sibelius Monument in Sibelius Park, Helsinki, was sculpted by the artist Eila Hiltunen. It was unveiled on the tenth anniversary of the maestro's death.

turn of the century a number of Finnish artists moved here and established an artists' colony. Some of them built their own homes, while others rented houses.

Seeking peace and quiet, Sibelius decided to move away from Helsinki to live among his artist friends near Tuusulanjärvi. However, since local landowners considered him to be a good-for-nothing with a drinking problem, he could not find a plot of land on which to build his house. Luckily things eventually worked out and in 1904 Aino and Jean Sibelius moved into their new house which they named Ainola. The house was designed by the architect Lars Sonck who at that time was also working on the designs for the most beautiful church in Finland, Tampere Cathedral.

The importance of the wise Aino Sibelius in her husband's life and work cannot be overestimated. The house, Ainola, has been preserved exactly as it was when Aino died in 1969. The grand piano and the waffle irons are still in situ, paintings by their artist friends still hang on the walls. Even the door to the study, the maestro's favourite place in the whole house, has been left ajar.

The death of Jean Sibelius is surrounded by tragic mystery. He died at Ainola at the very moment when the Fifth Symphony, which is considered to be the most optimistic of all his compositions, was being performed in the Festival Hall at the University of Helsinki.

In 1916, at about the time Sibelius finished his Fifth Symphony, he wrote in his diary: "I saw cranes. Once again, I heard my own voices." Forty-one years later, in September 1957, Sibelius was taking his morning walk near Ainola. On his return he said to his wife: "There they come, the birds of my youth." On that cloudy day the cranes were flying so low that Sibelius could see them plainly. Suddenly one of the birds broke away from the flock, flew towards Sibelius and circled above Ainola. The crane then continued on its journey, calling loudly.

Two days later Sibelius died while the strains of his Fifth Symphony were broadcast live over the radio. In Ainola, however, no one dared to listen.

The magnificent landscapes at Koli in Northern Karelia were a source of inspiration for Sibelius whose compositions often conjure up a powerful impression of nature.

Many visitors stop at Aino and Jean's plain gravestone in the garden at Ainola to pay silent homage to the great composer.

The Sibelius Museum, which is located near the old Turku Cathedral, has a great number of exhibits describing the life and works of the maestro. Indeed, one of the most popular sights in Helsinki is the Sibelius Monument in Sibelius Park in Töölö. The monument, which stands ten metres tall, was created in 1967 by the sculptor Eila Hiltunen.

Finland between Two Cultures

Since the Middle Ages the history and culture of Finland have been greatly influenced by the fact that the country is a kind of buffer zone between the cultures of east and west. In the eleventh century Finland was part of Sweden, which had a prominent presence in the west, whereas Novgorod (now Russia) in the east continually sought to expand its sphere of influence westwards, for example by propagating the Orthodox faith in Karelia.

In the early 1170s the Pope issued a papal bull stating that the Finns had been baptised into the Christian faith and were thus members of the Roman Catholic Church. Over the years Sweden and Novgorod waged a series of minor and major wars over the borders of Finland until the Treaty of Pähkinäsaari was signed in 1323. The treaty caused Finland to be divided into separate parts – east and west – in terms of government, religion and culture.

The centres of secular government were established at the castles of Turku, Hämeenlinna and Viipuri (now Vyborg). Powers and rulers changed over time and during the Kalmar Union (1397–1523) Finland was governed from Denmark, although the country was given a similar status in the union as the kingdoms of Sweden and Norway. At this time settlement spread eastward across the boundary laid down in the Pähkinäsaari Treaty and in 1475 construction of a castle in Savonlinna commenced to protect the settlers. All three castles have since become important venues for various cultural events.

During the reign of the great Swedish King Gustavus Vasa (1523–1560) the Reformation took place in Sweden, which consequently became a Protestant realm. Bishop Mikael Agricola, whose statue today stands in front of Turku Cathedral, had already translated the New Testament into Finnish in 1548. The birth of Finnish literature and of Finnish as a literary language is calculated from that year.

History continued with new kings and new wars. For 25 years Sweden waged war against Russia and managed to annex certain areas. However, the populace suffered and grew tired of being continually at war. Dissatisfaction finally erupted in Ostrobothnia, where

Today old hostilities are forgotten and you can travel quickly and comfortably by train from Helsinki to St. Petersburg and Moscow.

For hundreds of years Turku, the oldest city in Finland, and its 800-year-old cathedral have played an important part in Finland's history.

Uspensky Cathedral, Helsinki.

Between 1939 and 1945 Finland fought valiantly against the Soviet Union, but lost the war and had to cede sizeable areas in the north and south. In Suomussalmi close to the eastern border, at the end of the famous Raatteentie military road, there is a Border Guard Museum with an exhibition about the Winter War. Along the Raatteentie road there are many old battlegrounds.

peasants revolted in the Cudgel War which ran from 1596 to 1597. The name of the war has its origin in the fact that the peasants, led by Jaakko Ilkka, took arms (mainly cudgels) against the nobility. In the end both the Finnish peasants and the nobility suffered defeat. The nobles, who remained loyal to the king, managed to put down the peasant revolt but the new king, Carolus IX, repaid the nobility by executing some of its members for having sided with the wrong monarch.

Between 1713 and 1721 Russia occupied Finland and most of the upper classes fled to Sweden. The Great Northern War, which broke out in 1700, led to the collapse of Sweden. In the Treaty of Uusikaupunki Sweden ceded the south-eastern part of Finland to Russia. In 1703 Peter the Great founded his new capital, St. Petersburg, at the easternmost end of the Gulf of Finland. The fortress of Sveaborg (now Suomenlinna) was built outside Helsinki to guard against the Russians.

The population of Finland grew rapidly. Finland prospered economically, in spite of the wars against Russia, during the reign of Gustav III. International events finally halted the country's development. Sweden, under King Gustav IV Adolf, allied itself with the enemies of Napoleon, while Russia sided with France. The Russians attacked Finland and conquered the country in the War of Finland (1808–1809). Sweden was forced to surrender Finland up to the border running along the Tornionjoki River and Finland was annexed to the Russian Empire. The country was granted the status of an autonomous grand duchy, with its own central government administration, and was later transformed into the Imperial Senate of Finland.

In the nineteenth century Finnish culture and the nation's infrastructure developed rapidly. One reason for this was that the Russian emperors wanted to turn Helsinki into a Russified capital to offset the influence of the former capital, Turku, which had traditional ties with Sweden. In 1812 Helsinki was declared the new capital of the country and construction of the town began on a grand scale. However, in terms of its social structure, Finland remained a Scandinavian country throughout the nineteenth century.

Each of the Russian emperors brought his own set of principles to bear on the government of Finland. During the reign of Alexander II (1855–1881) Finland saw a series of unprecedented reforms. The *Diet* was convened, prosperity increased under liberal economic policies, Finnish-language schools were introduced and the number of newspapers increased. Finnish nationalism and liberal ideas gathered strength.

The reign of Alexander III signalled the start of a difficult period in Finland's history. The appointment by his successor, Nicholas II, of Nikolai Bobrikov as the new Governor General of Finland marked the beginning of Russian oppression in Finland in 1899. When the ultranationalist Bobrikov received dictatorial powers from the Emperor in 1903 he was assassinated by Eugen Schauman, a young clerk at the Board of Education. After shooting several rounds at Bobrikov, Schauman turned the gun on himself.

Emperor Nicholas II intended to put an end to Finland's special status within the empire and to annex the country to

White wooden crosses at the end of a small, grey *kropnitsa* in an Orthodox cemetery near the eastern border. *Kropnitsa* means 'the abode of the soul'.

Olavinlinna Castle in the city of Savonlinna was built as a defence against the Russians. Work on the castle was begun during the Kalmar Union in 1475 when Margaret, Queen of Denmark, was the ruler of Finland. Today the castle serves as the venue for a world-famous opera festival in the summertime and welcomes stars from the east as well as the west.

Russia on the same terms as the rest of the realm. Over 500,000 Finns signed a petition which was sent to the Emperor. Nevertheless, censorship was tightened and newspapers were closed down.

In 1891 Sibelius composed his Karelia Suite, the last movement of which he used for the composition entitled Finlandia. In the spring of 1900 the Helsinki Philharmonic Orchestra travelled to the World Exhibition in Paris where the Grand Duchy had its own pavilion designed by Finnish architects and artists. Sibelius had been asked to compose a 'furious' overture entitled Finlandia, but the maestro did not need to write a new piece as he already had a suitable composition. This work was to be Sibelius' own significant contribution to the Finnish struggle for independence.

The 1917 February Revolution in Russia put an end to imperial power and also ended the years of oppression in Finland. The October Revolution brought the Bolsheviks to power and Finland was declared a sovereign state in Helsinki. The *Diet* ratified the Declaration of Independence on 6th December 1917 and this date continues to be celebrated as Finland's Independence Day.

In 1939 the Soviet Union renounced its 1932 Non-aggression Pact with Finland. In November of the same year it launched the Winter War because Finland refused to grant the Soviets the concessions they had demanded. In the Treaty of Moscow in 1940 Finland surrendered the Karelian Isthmus and areas of Karelia adjoining Lake Ladoga as well as other areas further north. It also leased the Hanko Peninsula to the Soviets.

Finland now faced the problem of settling the Karelian refugees. When the former allies, Germany and the Soviet Union, decided to go to war against each other, the Finns sided with Germany and launched a new war in 1941. A massive attack by the Soviet Army in the summer of 1944 forced Finland to capitulate. The Germans retreated northwards from Finland towards Norway and destroyed almost all of Lapland on their way.

Under the Treaty of Paris in 1947 Finland had to surrender to the Soviets not only the areas surrendered in 1940, but also Petsamo in the north. War reparations, set at over three hundred million dollars, were paid by the Finns down to the very last cent.

Since World War II Finland has developed into one of the safest and most democratic states in the world, with an excellent system of social security similar to that in the other Scandinavian countries. In 1995 Finland became a member of the European Union and, at the beginning of 1999, it was the first country to join the European Monetary Union, one hour before every other nation.

Meet the Finns

The inhabitants of the six provinces of Finland have many distinctive characteristics.
As mentioned in the previous section on the country's history, Finland has been under the successive rule of either eastern or western powers. This historical fact has also left its mark on Finland's national character, its customs and culture. It is often said that Finns get their brains from the west but their hearts from the east and that they are different from their fellow Scandinavians. The Finns may be a bit shy and less talkative, but once they get to know you, you gain a trustworthy, lifelong friend. When it comes to strangers Finns like to keep their distance until they have got to know them better. At the same time, they are extremely friendly and hospitable people.

When speaking about the Finnish national character, the statesman J.V. Snellman (1806–1881), the father of the national awakening in Finland, would often quote a famous line by historian A.I. Arwidson: "We are not Swedes, we cannot become Russians, so let us be Finns!"

In the province of Åland (Ahvenanmaa) the majority of the population speaks Swedish and has a definite Swedish outlook.

Although Finnish lakes have no exotic fish, a diver can still find many other items of interest.

People in southern Finland are more international than the rest of the population, while those living along the western coast tend to be reserved and proud. The inhabitants of central Finland are relaxed and easy-going, and their dialect is perhaps the most beautiful of all dialects in Finland. In the east the influence of Russian and Karelian culture combined with the Greek Orthodox faith is reflected in people's attitudes. They are lively, hospitable folk and talk to strangers as if they were neighbours. Perhaps the friendliest people in Finland live in Kainuu: they are modest and uncomplicated, but also the poorest in the country. Life near the eastern border has always been more difficult than it is closer to affluent Sweden in the west.

The population of Lapland consists of the Lapps and non-indigenous Finns. Like all indigenous peoples, the Sami people are unique. One distinctive group of Finns lives in Savo in the eastern part of the country. They are called *piällysmiehet* (the bosses) by other Finns because they have more than their fair share of self-confidence! Their dialect can be difficult to understand, especially since it is coupled with

In Finland only families and close friends go to the sauna together. Taking a sauna is an ancient ritual during which you relax quietly and enjoy the soothing heat.

an idiosyncratic manner of speech. If you ask someone in Savo if it's going to rain, the answer will probably be "It may, but then again, it may not." Your guess is as good as mine!

People in the provinces speak their own dialects, whereas the Lapps have their own language. People from Helsinki can find it difficult to understand the Karelian dialect. Similarly, a tourist with a smattering of Finnish may be completely lost in the provinces where local dialects are totally incomprehensible, at least to a foreigner.

Religion is another important factor which makes for Finnish diversity. Eighty-five per cent of the Finnish population belongs to the Lutheran Church and about one per cent to the Orthodox Church. The rest either belong to no church at all, or to one of a number of smaller denominations. Although the number of Orthodox believers is fairly small, they are among the most visible groups of the Finnish population and many celebrities and professional people in the entertainment business have converted to the Orthodox faith.

Every Finn knows how to swim and fish.

In the summertime Finns wash their carpets on the shore. They don't do this to entertain the tourists. It is simply because it is the best way to clean carpets. This is an age-old ritual in Finland, although environmentally-friendly detergents are used today.

Old hay barns are still found in many places in the Finnish countryside. The games played differ from those played in city courtyards.

The blue cross on the Finnish flag reflects the blue waters of the lakes.

There are about 200,000 lakes in Finland and about half of the population spends the summer at the lakeside. Fish and sausages are grilled on outdoor barbecues. Even later on in the autumn many people still go for a dip in the lake after taking a sauna. The lakes are also used by ships to ferry local people and tourists over their blue waters.

National Parks – Gateways to Nature

The capercaillie, *Tetrao urogallus*, inhabits the coniferous forests of Finland. The males live alone for most of the year apart from during the mating season in the spring, when they spread their tail feathers, let their wings droop to the ground and make strange noises to attract the hens.

There are over thirty national parks in Finland. Three of these parks are run by the Forest Research Institute, while the others are run by the Forest and Park Service. Many of them are popular places for recreation and hiking. The parks also provide visitors with guidance and instruction on how to take care of the natural environment, as well as information on how to make the most of their visit.

Many parks now feature nature trails and information boards to point out places of special interest. There are also more than a dozen special nature centres which are like windows that open on Finnish nature. In addition to advice for hikers, the centres provide guidance and information about the terrain, as well as a number of other services.

The purpose of the parks is to preserve sites featuring special soils, flora or fauna which are specific to Finland. The parks contain many fantastic natural phenomena, such as rapids and gorges. Sites with outstandingly picturesque scenery or panoramic views have also been selected for preservation. In other places the aim has been to preserve landscapes affected by human habitation and culture, such as slash-and-burn clearings and natural meadows with old buildings. The national parks attract hundreds of thousands of visitors each year. Anyone may wander freely inside the parks, provided that they follow certain rules.

Most parks provide cooking areas and tent sites. Some even boast a camping site, well-equipped cottages or even wilderness huts for hire. Firewood is provided free of charge.

The first national parks were established in 1938. Most of them were lost after World War II when the borders were moved westward, although the Pyhätunturi and Pallas-Ounastunturi National Parks in Lapland still belong to Finland.

The national parks in southern Finland are busiest in the summer, while the northern parks attract visitors particularly in the winter and early spring, when the pristine snow provides excellent opportunities for skiing.

The most popular national parks are Nuuksio, some thirty kilometres from the capital, Oulanka and the more northerly Urho Kekkonen. Koli is also now a Finnish national park.

Nuuksio National Park is one of the few remaining wilderness areas in the south of Finland. The park is

There are still bears in several of the national parks. They are wary of people and sense their presence with ease. Consequently, they either stay well hidden or run away.

Trails winding among ancient trees take the hiker through many delightful settings.

characterised by all types of protected forests, as well as small lakes, ponds and streams. It is also a popular place for hiking. The landscape in Nuuksio is dominated by tall rocky outcrops and tree-covered hills which are dotted with dozens of lakes and ponds of various sizes. On the lakes you may catch sight of two species of protected birds – the red-throated diver and the osprey. Another protected bird, the nightjar, lives in the pine forest. Nuuksio has adopted the flying squirrel as its protected species. These acrobatic creatures glide from tree to tree with lightning speed. Nightfall sees them emerge from their nests in hollow trees.

The boreal forests of Oulanka National Park are situated in the Kuusamo-Salla region. The famous rapids and waterfalls along the big rivers fill the air with their thundering roar. Oulanka is also the natural habitat of many predators, including bears and wolves. Karhunkierros (Bear's Ring), a 90-kilometre long hiking trail which follows the Oulanka and Kitka Rivers, is one of the most famous nature trails in Finland and has many outstanding sights along the way.

Urho Kekkonen National Park was named after the statesman and president of Finland. An avid fisherman and great lover of outdoor sports, he led

The great grey owl, *Strix nebulosa*, is a rare bird which inhabits the coniferous forests of the northern hemisphere. The great grey owl sometimes builds its nest on the ground.

the country for a quarter of a century. The park is situated in a magnificent fell landscape, with many marked trails criss-crossing the wilderness. Measuring 2,550km^2, Urho Kekkonen is one of the largest national parks, second only to Lemmenjoki in Lapland. Lemmenjoki National Park is covered in the chapter on Lapland.

Koli National Park is characterised by the wooded hills and eskers (glacial deposits) which are typical of the North Karelian landscape. Every Finn is familiar with the panoramic views from Koli. The highest point is Ukko-Koli (Old Man Koli) which rises 347 metres above sea level. The Koli landscape emerged from beneath the glacial ice some 9,000 years ago. Signs of the Ice Age include glaciated rocks marked with the grooves formed by the receding glacier.

The landscape at Koli was an important inspiration in the birth of Karelianism, a movement launched by Finnish artists, composers and writers in the 1890s. Karelianism was a romantic national philosophy which idealised everything about Karelia. It was also around this time that Koli first became a popular sightseeing destination.

Unless otherwise specified, the Finnish Right of Public Access, which allows anyone to pick berries, mushrooms and those flowers which are not subject to wildlife protection orders, also applies in national parks. Of course, it is up to each individual to decide whether flowers are more beautiful wilting in a vase or growing wild in the forest. Naturally, when you are a guest of the forest, you must respect the wishes of your host.

Untouched ancient trees tower silently over fields of cotton grass.

Lapland's Pyhätunturi National Park contains the remnants of ancient Sami sacrificial sites within its boundaries. The 7-kilometre long chain of fells (the highest peak is 540 metres) was a sacred place for the Sami. The park has a total of 35 kilometres of marked trails as well as accommodation facilities.

Koli National Park is the subject of many paintings, poems and compositions by some of the greatest Finnish artists. The first small guesthouse was built in Koli in 1896. The vistas which open up from the highest point in Koli are part of Finland's national heritage.

In the national parks you may pick berries and mushrooms, but flowers and plants are strictly protected. In the north, in particular, there are beautiful wide fields filled with cotton grass. The picture shows a species of cotton grass called *Eriophorum scheuchzeri*.

Oulanka National Park in Kuusamo is a unique river landscape. The park adjoins the Paanajärvi National Park to the east on the Russian side of the border.

If you go down to the woods today...

About a third of Finland is covered by forest. These forests are inhabited by about five hundred species of vertebrates, the biggest of which are the elk and the bear. In eastern Finland you can also find wolves and there are a few wolverines in the north. The lynx lives in the forests of southern Finland. Of course, the forests in Lapland teem with semi-domesticated reindeer. Badgers, foxes, rabbits, otters and beavers are also inhabitants of the Finnish forests.

The ringed seal is the most endangered seal species in the world and can only be found in parts of Lake Saimaa. It is also the only endemic mammal in Finland that is protected by both the Forest and Park Service and the World Wildlife Fund (WWF). The ringed seal and its nesting grounds are protected

Bears lead a quiet and carefree life in the depths of the Finnish wilderness.

A happy family of brown bears, *Ursus arctos*, observing tourists.

under the Wildlife Protection Act.

Finland's three zoos are all worth a visit. Ranua Zoo in the north contains mainly Arctic species, whereas Ähtäri Zoo in central Finland has domestic species. Both of these zoos cover a very large area and provide the animals with plenty of space to move around in. Korkeasaari Zoo in Helsinki is a favourite with visitors, especially families with young children. The zoo can be reached by boat from the Market Square.

You can see brown bears in all three zoos, but in the north and east you can also encounter them in the wild. Always remember that bears are even more wary of humans than we are of them.

The Finnish national bird is the whooper swan, *Cygnus cygnus*. It is a protected species whose loud whooping call can be heard from a great distance. The whooper swan nests in the northern parts of Finland.

In Ranua Zoo there are many semi-tame lynx which, contrary to popular belief, are not the same as wildcats. Some of the lynx in Ranua have been featured in films. The Latin name of the lynx is *Lynx lynx*.

The elk, *Alces alces*, is the most common forest animal in Finland. It wanders around the forests either alone or in family groups and is as wary of humans as the bear.

The reindeer is a semi-tame sub-species of the caribou. It can never be fully domesticated and lives half wild on the fells.

Colourful autumn in Finland

The Finnish word *ruska* means a forest glowing with autumn shades. In September, when the weather is often still quite warm, something strange can happen. When there has been an overnight frost the whole landscape is suddenly filled with red, orange and yellow shades in the morning. Although magnificent colours can be also found in the south, many people choose this time of year to go hiking in Lapland. Jack Frost also paints the trees and bushes in the parks of Helsinki with the same array of glowing colours.

Finland is Music

Matti Salminen is an acclaimed Finnish opera singer whose magnificent bass is often heard on the most prestigious opera stages of the world.

Finns are great lovers of music. As well as their own distinctive Finnish form of the tango, they enjoy all kinds of music. The numerous music festivals organised by this small nation attract an amazing number of people from all over the world every year.

Although Sibelius is the most widely-known figure in Finnish music, Finland can boast many talented musicians. The acclaimed singers Karita Mattila and Monica Groop, the world-famous conductor Esa-Pekka Salonen, the piano virtuoso Olli Mustonen, the composer Einojuhani Rautavaara and the crazy rock group Leningrad Cowboys are just a few examples of the musical talent Finland has given to the world.

In spite of its relatively small size, Finland hosts an extraordinarily large number of music festivals. What makes these Finnish music festivals stand out from the rest is a relaxed atmosphere with high quality music and famous performers.

In 1969 the cellist Seppo Kimanen, who was about 20 at the time, founded the Kuhmo Chamber Music Festival. Organised in the municipality of Kuhmo, which is more than twice the geographical size of Tokyo but has a population of just 13,000, this two-week musical event has become famous the world over. The festival programme, which centres on various themes, includes chamber music classics, famous ensembles and soloists. The event is also known as The Spirit of Kuhmo and is synonymous with surprises, humour and simplicity. In the Kuhmo concert hall, which has superb acoustics, musicians play in their shirtsleeves. In the evenings acclaimed soloists relax on the shores of the nearby lake. The music is enjoyed as much by the locals, who put their heart and soul into the organisation of the festival, as by the festival-goers themselves.

In Kuhmo time is music. Every year the white summer nights of Kainuu and the down-to-earth atmosphere of the event draw over a hundred musicians to the festival.

The Mikkeli Music Festival, held from the end of June to the beginning of July, is organised by Valery Gergiyev. In addition to being the festival's artistic director, this talented man is also one of the

The Kuhmo Chamber Music Festival has developed into one of the world's most popular chamber music events.

The Finns forget their shyness when they do the samba.

The national instrument of Finland is a type of zither called the *kantele*. It has been used for centuries to accompany folk songs.

most prestigious conductors in the world. Artists who tour the world throughout the year meet each other so seldom that Mikkeli is like a musician's paradise for them. This high-class event is also attended by Gergiyev's friends, including the viola virtuoso Yuri Bashmet, the pianist Alexandr Toradze (reputedly the best interpreter of Prokofiev) and many others, all of whom perform at the modern concert hall in Mikkeli.

Gergiyev rents a cottage for his circle of friends in a secret location. It is here that the mother of the chief conductor of the famous Mariinsky Theatre of St. Petersburg prepares good Finnish fare for her son and his friends. They are also free to enjoy the sauna and take a dip in the clear waters of the lake – in short, to enjoy typical Finnish summer life at its best.

The month-long Savonlinna Opera Festival attracts all kinds of people as well as famous opera stars. The festival is staged in Olavinlinna Castle and most of the productions are classical opera. The event in Savonlinna is the best-known and oldest music festival in Finland. The first Opera Festival was arranged in Savonlinna in 1912, with the famous Finnish soprano Aino Ackté as its artistic director. Modern, large-scale productions have been staged in Savonlinna since 1967.

Olavinlinna Castle was built in 1476 by Erik Axelsson-Tott, the regent of Sweden, to protect the eastern border of the realm. The foundations of the castle were laid on a rocky island in the middle of a river. The town of Savonlinna grew up around the castle and its municipal status was officially acknowledged in 1639. There is also a historical museum section in Olavinlinna Castle.

The Heta Music Festival, held in Lapland

There are often more spectators than dancers at the popular street dances which are held in Turku during the summer.

274
562

during Easter, is the northernmost music festival in the European Union. Church and baroque music are performed against the backdrop of snowy fells provided by the region.

The AVANTI! Summersounds festival is held in Porvoo at the end of June. It was founded by conductor Esa-Pekka Salonen and his friends who are still responsible for organising the festival programme.

The Imatra Big Band Festival, which is held in late June/early July, is the only festival in the world dedicated to big band jazz. Every year about 100,000 visitors flock to the Pori Jazz Festival to listen to world-class jazz, both old and new. The Kaustinen Folk Music Festival, held in July, is dedicated to folk music from all over the world. The Kaustinen festival is a place where virtuoso musicians are seen as well as heard, and where the colourful, exotic atmosphere is almost palpable.

If you want to get to know the Finnish soul, the Seinäjoki Tango Festival, which is held in July, is the place to go. Unlike their western neighbours, Finns have no royalty to admire, so every year they elect a tango queen and king in Seinäjoki. Many of the winners of the contest have carved successful careers for themselves in the entertainment business. In Seinäjoki anyone can dance the tango from morning till night or perhaps just learn the first steps of the dance that is so close to the Finnish heart.

When the Soviet Union collapsed and became Russia once more a famous Finnish rock group came up with the idea of changing its name to Leningrad Cowboys. They invited the Alexandrov Choir of the Red Army from Moscow to join them and since then they have toured the world extensively, entertaining people with their crazy hairdos and pointed shoes.

Finnish Cuisine

Cloudberries picked in the northern forests are used to make delicious jam.

Finnish cuisine is a blend of eastern and western influences. Scandinavian fish delicacies, pies from Karelia and Russia, mushrooms and bread form the basis of Finnish cuisine. Wild berries are used to prepare succulent desserts.

The Finnish food year begins with Shrovetide. The table is laden with blintzes and the roe of small whitefish which are eaten with sour cream and raw onion. Many people consider Scandinavian roe to be superior to Russian caviar. Dessert traditionally consists of Shrove buns filled with marzipan.

The most traditional Easter foods are eggs and *mämmi*, a special Finnish delicacy made of rye flour and malt and enjoyed with a sprinkling of sugar and milk. An Easter dish which has been borrowed from Russia is *pasha*, a sweet dessert made from cream, butter and quark.

The traditional May Day delicacies are mead and fritters, while Midsummer is celebrated with delicious fish dishes served with new potatoes. August signals the beginning of the crayfish season. Finnish freshwater crayfish are among the most delicious shellfish in the world. When they are in season it's time for crayfish parties with shots of vodka accompanied by drinking songs.

Finns flock to the forests to gather mushrooms and berries in the late summer and early autumn. The taste of bilberries, lingonberries and cloudberries can then be stored and savoured throughout the winter and spring months.

Finnish vegetables and home-grown berries have an exquisite taste. The secret is the Finnish summer which only lasts about three months. During half of that time the sun shines practically 24 hours a day and as the potatoes and berries ripen they acquire a strong, delicious flavour.

Finnish Christmas fare includes herring in various forms, beetroot/herring pickle, casseroles made with potato, swede or carrot, and baked ham, although nowadays turkey often replaces the ham. The traditional dessert is prune compote.

In Finland the oven is frequently used to prepare traditional Finnish cuisine and indeed the Finns bake some of the best bread in the world. Bread-baking, a skill discovered over 6,000 years ago, is one of the oldest ways of making food from cereals. The first bakeries were established in Finland a couple of hundred years ago and today bread is baked in roughly a thousand bakeries across the country. Finnish rye bread is deservedly famous, particularly since medical studies have shown that it can help prevent certain illnesses.

Finnish beer and especially vodka are renowned all over the world but there are also some fine liqueurs made from Finnish berries. However, the healthiest drink is pure, clean water and you can drink it quite safely straight from the tap even in the most modest of Finland's guesthouses.

Every province has its own special dishes which are worth trying. Sometimes you may need to pluck up some courage to taste the strange-looking foods, but you are usually more than pleasantly surprised.

There are plenty of bilberries, lingonberries and other berries to be found in Finnish forests.

There are excellent hunting grounds in Finland. Tourist companies at the eastern border arrange organised fishing and hunting excursions to hunting grounds teeming with game on the Russian side of the border.

One distinctive way of enjoying delicious Finnish unripened cheese is to cook it over an open fire. This kind of cheese is called 'bread cheese' or 'cheese bread' depending on the region.

Slowly grilled over an open fire, fresh fish fillets are a deliciously crisp delicacy.

A Kainuu banquet table is laden with an abundance of freshwater fish prepared in countless ways: fish pastries, salmon cakes, salted and smoked delicacies.

Savu Ahven file

Finland is Glass Country

The better-known history of Finnish glass begins in 1793 when a glassworks was founded in Nuutajärvi. Glass had been manufactured in Finland since 1681, but the first glass factory only exists in the history books. In the late eighteenth century people began demanding bigger windows with double panes and this meant that glass production had to be increased. Glass was also needed for bottles to hold spirits and jars were needed for jam and fruit juice. The increased demand led to the founding of the Nuutajärvi glassworks.

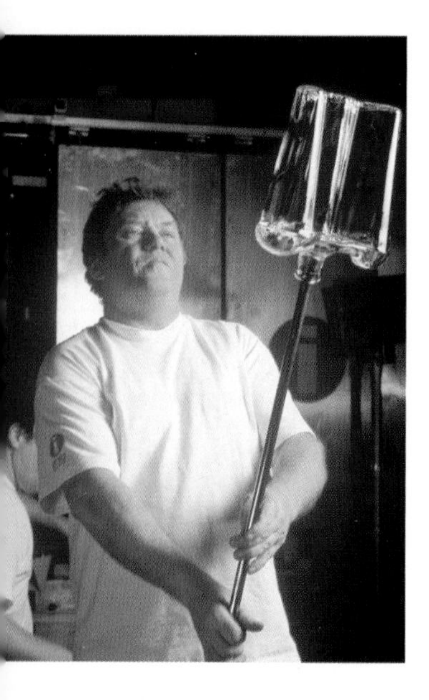

A glass-blower inspecting an Aalto vase at Iittala.

The Nuutajärvi works became international in the 1850s when several glass-blowers were hired from Germany, Belgium and France. The director of the works was brought in from a crystal factory in Sèvres and the accountant was one G.F. Stockmann from Germany. He turned out to be an excellent businessman and later founded the Stockmann's department store in Helsinki which is still the most famous and the finest department store in Finland.

The rise of Nuutajärvi glass to international fame was largely due to the efforts of the designer Kaj Franck who was appointed artistic director of the works in the 1950s. Whilst Finland was still recovering from the war the award-winning designs of Franck and other great Finnish glass designers, such as Timo Sarpaneva and Tapio Wirkkala, helped to spread the word about the country.

Although it is not quite as old as Nuutajärvi, the glass-producing town of Iittala is the birthplace of many famous designs, including Sarpaneva's acclaimed i-line of modern utility glassware. All the artists who have worked at Iittala have designed utility items as well as art glass and all have emphasised the fact that their work would not have been possible without the talents of the glass-blowers. Visitors to the glassworks can see the glass-blowers at work every day of the week.

The most famous article to have come from Iittala is without a doubt a vase designed by Alvar Aalto. The vase has a story behind it. In 1936 the Karhula-Iittala glassworks announced a competition for new glass designs to be exhibited at the World Exhibition in Paris. The first prize went to an eccentric vase design with the peculiar name – Eskimo Woman's Leather Breeches. The designer was a young architect called Alvar Aalto who was rewarded with a small sum of money. The glassworks in turn obtained permanent rights to the production of the Aalto vase. The factory has never published any figures which would reveal how many millions of Aalto vases it has made over the years.

Both glass-producing towns also have museums, factory shops, temporary exhibitions and cafeterias for visitors to enjoy.

The Finnish Glass Museum is situated in Riihimäki. The objects in the museum were originally collected by students of the University of Helsinki in the 1950s; a decade of exceptional creative talent in Finland. The students managed to collect some five hundred items which formed the basic collection of the museum when it was founded in 1961. The museum is housed in the beautiful old Riihimäki glassworks and was renovated using designs by Tapio Wirkkala. A new section was opened in 1981 on the 300th anniversary of Finnish glass-making.

The Savoy vase, designed by Alvar Aalto in 1936, is considered to be one of the milestones in Finnish design.

Swedish-speaking Åland

The island has many hiding places, such as these sculpture-like crevices at Källskärskannan.

The autonomous province of Åland, with its thousands of islands, straits and wide expanses of open sea, is one of the most beautiful seascapes in the world. The history of its habitation goes back 6,000 years when hunters and fisherfolk first moved to the islands. Åland, too, has been conquered many times in the past. Countries fighting for its possession have included Sweden, Norway, Russia, England and France.

The Treaty of Paris of 1856 stipulated that no armies could ever be stationed in Åland. In 1921 the League of Nations ratified the demilitarisation of the islands and also decreed that Åland would henceforth belong to Finland, which in turn pledged to preserve the language and culture of the Swedish-speaking population. Åland has its own flag and its own postal service which serves a population of about 25,000 people living on 65 islands.

Åland is a paradise for anglers and sometimes the local fishermen take people along on their fishing trips.

One of the most interesting museums in Åland is the hunting and fishing museum, *Ålands jakt- och fiskemuseum.* The exhibits in the grey museum building in Käringsund tell fascinating tales about life on the islands in the olden days, including stories about seal hunting and the important role of women in the various stages of fishing. On the shore there are old boathouses which have been bleached by the years.

Åland is also a haven for nature lovers. The meadows are filled with countless varieties of flowers in the summer months. The bird on Åland's crest is the sea eagle and, if you are lucky, you may see this huge bird of prey and hear its call as it hovers in the sky, along with other protected bird species. There are over a dozen nature sanctuaries in Åland. Deer can be

The islands and beaches of Åland are a veritable summer paradise.

seen prancing gracefully in the forests and sometimes, to the astonishment of tourists, mute swans may flock in their hundreds to the bay next to airport in the capital, Mariehamn.

Ships and shipping have always been part of everyday life in Åland. Marienhamn is the home port of the giant Viking Line ferries which plough the sea lanes between Finland and Sweden. The port was also home to the world's largest fleet of sailing ships at the turn of the century. Three-masted and four-masted barques used to make the long trip from Marienhamn to the corn markets of England and Australia.

The interior of the Maritime Museum resembles the deck of a sailing ship. Once inside, you get a good idea of what life was like for seafarers in the past when the profession was fraught with danger. The four-masted steel barque, *Pommern*, is moored at the quay next to the museum. The ship was built in Scotland and was converted into a museum ship in 1952.

Among the most valuable sites of cultural heritage in Åland are the dozens of mediaeval stone churches, many of which date back to the twelfth and thirteenth centuries. The historical value of the churches, each with its own patron saint, is enhanced by their beautiful paintings and sculptures.

Stunted pines and low juniper bushes grow on the Åland islands. Juniper is protected throughout Finland.

The archipelago glows with shades of yellow and gold in the autumn.

The Beginnings of Finland

Food lovers consider Turku Market Hall, which is over a hundred years old, to be one of the best places to buy food in Finland.

The oldest and historically the richest area of Finland is the former province of Varsinais-Suomi. The south-western part of Finland has the most fertile arable land in the country because of its favourable maritime climate and its forests are dominated by broad-leaved deciduous trees. Thousands of years ago travelling merchants used to come here frequently to buy furs and fish, and to sell salt, wine, silver and gold. The centre of commerce was the Aurajoki River which runs through Turku, the oldest city in Finland.

Finnish mediaeval stone churches bear witness to the long history of Finnish culture and its connections with Europe. In the Middle Ages the Baltic Sea was Finland's link with the rest of the world and new trends in the arts often reached its shores via ships coming from Germany. Finland boasts over a hundred mediaeval stone churches, most of which are located in the south-western part of the country.

Visitors can take the Tour of the Seven Churches which gives them an excellent opportunity to discover some of Finland's mediaeval treasures. The tour, which starts at Turku, includes a visit to Louhisaari Castle where the famous Finnish general, Field-Marshal C.G.E. Mannerheim (1867–1951), was born. Mannerheim served in the Russian imperial army until 1917. He then commanded the Finnish government's troops in Finland's War of Independence in 1918, served as the Commander-in-Chief of the Finnish army against the Soviet Union in World War II and in the difficult years from 1944 to 1946 he served as the President. Some years on Mannerheim settled in Switzerland where he later died. Mannerheim is Finland's most famous and celebrated statesman.

Turku was founded in 1229. It was the cultural and administrative centre of Finland until 1827 when a great fire burned nearly all of the town to the ground. After the fire the balance of power changed and Turku lost its status as the most important town in the country to Helsinki which had already been made the official capital in 1812.

Turku Castle was built at about the same time as the town itself. John, Duke of Finland and the favourite son of King Gustavus I Vasa, held a sumptuous court in the castle. In 1562 John brought his young wife, the Polish princess Catherine, to Turku. Catherine brought with her a sizeable dowry and dozens of courtiers who introduced the townspeople to new and strange habits, such as the use of napkins and forks.

Turku Castle was converted into a history museum in 1881. Wars had ravaged the buildings and restoration was not completed until 1993. Since then the castle, with its 160 rooms, has been recounting tales of important people and events in Turku and Finland. Nowadays historical banquets are organised in the castle at Christmas time. They range from a Christmas feast for the poor to sumptuous Renaissance banquets, all in the style of Catherine's court.

Aboa Vetus et Ars Nova (Old Turku and New Art), which opened its doors in the early 1990s, is an interesting museum. It stands on the banks of the Aurajoki River in the grand residence formerly belonging to the family of von Rettig, a rich tobacco manufacturer. When storage rooms for the collection of paintings were being excavated in the basement the workers discovered an old cobbled street of a nunnery dating back some 400 years. Although it was known that the site had been inhabited since the twelfth century, the discovery of over 30,000 artefacts buried in the ground was very significant. Multimedia presentations and the objects on display enable visitors to learn about life in Turku in the olden days. Visitors can also enjoy modern art on the upper floors of the museum.

The great fire of Turku, started by a maid's carelessness, burned the entire town to the ground except for a few stone houses. The only exception was an area of wooden homes called Luostarinmäki which was situated far away from the town's centre. The area's inhabitants were poor artisans and mostly first-generation town-dwellers who kept domestic animals in small sheds. People who had lost their homes in the fire temporarily moved to Luostarinmäki as tenants until they could build new homes.

Luostarinmäki was peaceful and quiet until it was converted into a handicraft museum in 1940. The chief attraction of the museum is its authenticity. The artisans who were still living there in 1940 were allowed to stay in residence and their homes have been preserved in their original state. In the summer the museum organises demonstrations of the late artisans' work.

Turku Cathedral is the most valuable ecclesiastical building in Finland and a shrine of national importance. The cathedral was consecrated in the 1290s by which stage it had already acquired its present form. Centuries of wars and plundering, as well as various renovations, have left their mark on the building. Several famous people are buried in the cathedral. Some of the cathedral's art treasures are on display in a museum which is separate from the rest of the building. The cathedral's surroundings along the banks of the Aurajoki River include one of the oldest parts of Turku which boasts fine parks and old architecture.

Not far from Turku lies the small and idyllic summer town of Naantali. In 1443 the construction of a Birgittine convent was begun in Naantali. The work was supervised by the main convent of the Order of Saint Birgitta in Vadstena in Sweden. Since 1924 the call to vespers has rung out every summer's evening from the church steeple

Finland was governed from Turku Castle for several centuries, until in 1881 it was converted into a provincial museum comprising just one room. Today all the 160 rooms of the historical castle are open to the public.

The popular Moomin Valley is a tourist attraction which blends well with the small picturesque town of Naantali.

The Aurajoki River, which flows through Turku, is a popular summer attraction.

after the clock strikes eight.

Today the main tourist attraction in Naantali is Moomin Valley, a park modelled on the Moomin books by Finnish author Tove Jansson. The park has a real Moomin House with live characters from the Moomin books to entertain children and grown-ups alike.

Along the Old King's Road

The lantern room can only be reached by climbing 252 steps.
The beacon is operated by wind power.

In the Middle Ages envoys of the Crown, merchants, messengers and affluent burghers used to cross the sea from Stockholm to Turku and then continue on to St. Petersburg on horseback. Roadside manors, inns, taverns and lodging houses sprang up to serve the travellers who also included kings and emperors. Known as the King's Road, it was the most important thorough-fare in Scandinavia, stretching all the way from Norway through Sweden, Åland and southern Finland to St. Petersburg. The road has recently undergone something of a revival, especially since the old churches, manors, mill communities and part of the old road network are still in existence.

The Billnäs ironworks in the municipality of Pohja is the oldest private ironworks surviving to this day. Carl Billsten, the Swedish mining master, commissioned the construction of the Billnäs ironworks community on the lower reaches of Karjaanjoki River in 1641. Five years later he founded the Fagervik ironworks in Inkoo.

Over the centuries the ironworks changed hands and went through both good times and bad. In the late eighteenth century, however, the Fagervik works prospered under the ownership of the Stockholm-born Hisinger brothers, so much so that King Gustav III of Sweden once stayed with the two brothers at their manor. Another king, Gustav IV Adolf, visited the Billnäs ironworks in 1796 on his way to St. Petersburg. The purpose of his journey was to propose to Alexandra, the granddaughter of Empress Catherine II, but she refused him.

Workers' dwellings along the main street in Billnäs have been preserved almost in their original state and the main street in Fagervik, which is lined with red houses, is equally as charming.

The ironworks at Fiskars was founded in 1649 by a merchant from Turku called Peter Thorwöste. However, large-scale industrial production did not begin there until Johan Julin, a mighty merchant from Turku, bought the works in 1822. Fiskars is still owned by Julin's descendants and the Fiskars name is famous throughout the world as a manufacturer of quality scissors.

In 1983 the Fiskars community was bought by the Pohja municipality and then developed into a popular residential area for artists, as well as a tourist attraction with several museums, shops and cafés. However, the chief attractions in Fiskars are the extensive themed exhibitions which are organised every summer. Some of the forty or more residential artists in Fiskars run their own art galleries.

The Mustio ironworks was founded in the sixteenth century to refine iron ore. Since the mid-eighteenth century (except for a period between 1940 and 1985) the factory and its manor have been owned by the Linder family. The priceless wall paintings and interior decorations in the main house dating from 1792 have been restored with the help of the National Board of Antiquities. Famous guests at the manor have included the Russian Emperors, Alexander I and II.

There is a mystery associated with the Mustio manor. King Gustav III of Sweden was staying in the manor while it was still under construction in 1788. He was determined to continue the hopeless war against Russia, even though a hundred officers in his army had demanded that he make peace. Despite punishing the officers by hanging one of them, the war did not end until 1790. Since that time the halls of the manor are said to have been haunted by the ghost of King Gustav III.

The park and buildings at Mustio are all carefully tended. In the summer the manor serves as the venue for popular antique fairs.

Hanko is the southernmost town in Finland. It stands on a promontory surrounded by the sea on three sides and is graced with sandy beaches that extend for miles. The harbour in Hanko was known to sailors as far back as the thirteenth century and Hanseatic merchants used to rest there on their way to Russia. Today Hanko is one of the most popular seaside towns in Finland, with a charming town centre and hundreds of visiting leisure boats in its marina.

Hauensuoli (meaning pike's intestine) got its name from a narrow strait separating two small islands just outside Hanko. The islands are among the most important sites of cultural and historical significance in Finland. The rocks, smoothed by glaciers, have served as the 'guestbook of the islands' since the fifteenth century and have provided welcome shelter for vessels waiting for the weather to improve. The passengers and captains used to draw, write and carve their crests and names on the rocks to while away the time. There are some 640 images and original inscriptions at Hauensuoli, including the names of such famous figures as the Swedish kings Erik XIV, John III and Gustav III.

Built in 1906, the lighthouse at Bengtskär is only a couple of hours' boat ride from Hanko. The lighthouse's tower rises 52 metres above the surrounding sea like a magnificent monument. Over the centuries scores of seafarers, ranging from Vikings to Hanseatic merchants, have sailed by this rocky island. The sea around the island is riddled with submerged rocks and the seabed is littered with shipwrecks. At first the Russian authorities refused to allow a lighthouse to be built. However, after a small steamer sank on the rocks in 1905, taking with it six passengers, the tall lighthouse was soon built within a year. Made of granite taken from the island, 120 workmen were needed to complete its construction.

The lighthouse is now a popular tourist attraction. Visitors can climb the 252 steps up the spiral staircase to the round lantern room at the top. The large prism is still in working order and refracts the light of the evening sun in a thousand colours. The beacon in the lighthouse is powered by electricity generated by wind power.

Before World War II broke out there were still several families living in the lighthouse. The last lighthouse keeper moved to the mainland when the beacon was automated in 1968. Today the lighthouse boasts a museum as well as a small chapel and temporary exhibitions. Visitors can also stay overnight in the lighthouse, take a sauna and enjoy a meal. The rocky island is barren of trees, but the crags are filled with the splendour of wild flowers throughout the summer months.

Bengtskär lighthouse towers 52 metres above the sea.

Big car ferries are not alone in the water. Sailing boats are also a popular means of travelling along the southern coast.

Romantic Porvoo

Old Porvoo is an exceptionally attractive area. Its crowning glory is the 15th-century Porvoo Cathedral.

Porvoo was founded in 1383 and is the second oldest town in Finland after Turku. In the Middle Ages it was an important staging post on the King's Road, also known as the Great Coastway. Following the annexation of Finland to Russia in 1809, Porvoo was brought to Europe's attention when Emperor Alexander I convened the *Diet* there. This was an important event in Finland's history: the meeting of the estates was a signal that the Russian conqueror was willing to respect Finland's rights in spite of the annexation of Finland to the empire.

Alexander attended the *Diet* in person and it is rumoured that a romance sprang up between the Emperor and a pretty Finnish maiden named Ulla Möllersvärd. The romance is said to have all started in the great hall of the grammar school by the church square which has survived to this day. The square is home to another historic building, the impressive Porvoo Cathedral, which was built in the fifteenth century. It was here that Alexander made his promise to respect the religion and fundamental laws of Finland.

Most of Old Porvoo, with its picturesque alleys and wooden houses, was built after the fire of 1760. The 240 houses remaining from that time now have protected status. Porvoo is only an hour's drive from Helsinki and it has become a popular place for daytrippers who are staying in the capital. In summer Porvoo can also be reached via the beautiful archipelago on an old steamer named after Finland's national poet, Johan Ludvig Runeberg (1804–1877). A museum was opened in Runeberg's home in Porvoo in 1880. Runeberg and his wife, Frederika, moved to the house in 1852 and they lived there for the rest of their lives, even though Runeberg was bedridden for the last 14 years of his life. In 1846 the poet wrote the Swedish lyrics to Maamme, the Finnish national anthem. Frederika, who was also a writer, died at home in 1879 just two years after her husband. The house has been preserved exactly as it was at the time of Frederika's death.

Porvoo was finally placed on the map in 1809 when Alexander I, Emperor of Russia and Grand Duke of the autonomous Grand Duchy of Finland, convened the Diet there.

The Happy Life of an Imperial Family

One of the attractions along the old King's Road is the imperial fishing lodge at Langinkoski. Prince Alexander of Russia paid a visit to the lower reaches of the Kymijoki River in 1880 to try the salmon fishing. The roar of the rapids, the exquisite scenery and the great salmon catches stayed in his mind. By the time he returned to Langinkoski in 1884 with his wife Maria Fyodorovna, formerly Princess Dagmar of Denmark, Alexander had become Emperor. Dagmar was initially engaged to his brother Nicholas, but when Nicholas died Alexander became Emperor against his will. The imperial couple's sympathetic subjects built the lodge for them and granted the Emperor perpetual fishing rights to the rapids.

The imperial couple led a simple life at Langinkoski. The Emperor chopped wood with a Finnish axe made at the Billnäs ironworks, carried water to the kitchen and firewood to the stove on which the Empress would cook salmon soup. However, the housewarming party they gave in 1889 was far from modest. It was attended by the Queen of Greece, the Duchess of Edinburgh and many other famous names from the Grand Duchy and Russia.

Alexander III had a deep love of his family, of nature and of Finland. When he died in 1894 his son Nicholas II succeeded him to the throne. Nicholas, however, showed no interest in Langinkoski. The dowager Empress Dagmar never returned there and she donated the lodge to the Red Cross in World War I.

The rooms of the two-storey lodge are preserved as they were in Alexander's time. The lodge was converted into a museum in 1933 and present-day royalty visiting Finland often come to the lodge to marvel at the imperial modesty of the place.

On this porch Dagmar, the former princess of Denmark, sat watching her husband Emperor Alexander III catch huge salmon from the rapids running past the house.

HAMINA - AN OCTAGONAL FORTRESS TOWN

The streets lead away from the octagonal plaza of Hamina and end at the walls which surround the town.

Hamina is a city which has been on both sides of the international border at various times in its history. The city has an amazingly disciplined construction plan dating from the 1720s. A renaissance-style town hall, built in 1798, stands on its central octagonal plaza. The eight streets, which lead away from the plaza, are intersected by two orbital roads and the entire city centre is surrounded by a well-preserved city wall which is almost three kilometres long.

There are several museums in the city centre and, as Hamina is an old fortress town, many of these are dedicated to military history. It is all the more surprising, therefore, that the best-known statue in the city in Kadettikoulunkatu Street is not a memorial to some great war hero, but a statue of Varvara Schant erected by a reserve officer training corps. Varvara (1870–1941) was a doughnut and pie merchant who delighted the young soldiers by following them with his wares, even when they were on manoeuvres over open terrain.

The region of Kymenlaakso, where Hamina is located, also contains one of Finland's four UNESCO World Cultural Heritage sites – the Verla mill in Jaala, with its foundry village and the director's residence. The site was converted into a mill museum and opened to the public in 1972. The buildings date back to 1885 and comprise one of Finland's few old mill complexes which have survived intact. In its day the complex was an important mechanical wood pulp and paper mill. The interiors and machinery of the mill are still on display together with examples of the work which was carried out there.

The nearby municipality of Valkeala has another attraction in the form of the prehistoric rock paintings which are thousands of years old.

The Home of Three Architects

The Art Nouveau country home of Hvitträsk is one of the masterpieces of Finnish architecture. Once the home of several creative people, it is now a museum open to the public.

Kirkkonummi is about half an hour's drive from Helsinki to the west. Here, on the shores of Lake Hvitträsk, stands a country home which has passed into the annals of world architectural history. The building was designed in 1902–1903 by three young Finnish architects who had won acclaim in international competitions: Eliel Saarinen, Herman Gesellius and Armas Lindgren. A good friend of the architects, the composer Jean Sibelius, had recommended the site when spending a summer there. The building was a log construction on a stone foundation. Its national romantic style also contained a dash of Karelian influence, as the leading Finnish artists of the late nineteenth century spent a good deal of time in the birthplace of the Kalevala in search of their soul and cultural roots. There is, however, a good deal of the English country estate in the Hvitträsk design. The interiors also show the influence of Finnish peasant architecture and mediaeval stone churches with their imposing vaulted arches.

Eliel Saarinen was the most famous of the three architects. He lived at Hvitträsk until 1923 when he emigrated to the USA. His best-known American works include the Cranbrook Academy of Art in Michigan. Saarinen became a leading figure at Cranbrook, turning the Academy into the leading American centre for modern architecture and design.

Saarinen pursued his work in the USA with his son, Eero, who was also an architect. The Saarinens continued to spend their summers at Hvitträsk until the 1940s.

There was an element of scandal surrounding the private lives of the three architects in their early years at Hvitträsk. Eliel Saarinen lived with his wife, Mathilda, in the main building. Herman Gesellius lived with his sister, Louise, in one of the annexes. After a couple of years this arrangement changed: Eliel married Louise and Herman married Mathilda. Armas Lindgren, unable to tolerate such impropriety, moved to Helsinki. After the Saarinens' departure Hvitträsk fell into less respectful hands. It was finally purchased by the Finnish State in 1981 and the original interiors of the house were restored. Today Hvitträsk is a museum and the most important of its thirty-two rooms is the huge studio in which the architects worked together to design many of Helsinki's Art Nouveau buildings. Saarinen's best-known works from this period include the Helsinki Central Railway Station (1906–1914). All three architects were born in the mid-1870s. Eliel Saarinen died in 1950, Herman Gesellius in 1916 and Armas Lindgren in 1929.

The Oldest Brick Buildings in Finland

Finland's oldest brick building, Tavastehus, contains one of the country's finest cultural history museums.

The people of Häme, who still have a reputation for being strong-willed, were the last to surrender to the Christianisation of Finland and the spread of Swedish rule. The faith, heavy taxes and new prohibitions imposed in the thirteenth century finally angered them so much that they rose up in rebellion. Once again the Pope had to issue a papal bull to express his indignation at the people of Häme for turning back into heathens.

The mighty forefather of the Folkunga family, Birger Jarl, who was the founder of Stockholm and the de facto ruler of Sweden under a weak king, launched a crusade against the people of Häme under papal orders and crushed them. Hämeenlinna Castle was built as a defence against Novgorod and the re-Christianised people of Häme were grateful to Birger who put an end to their slavery under the rule of Novgorod.

Construction work on the castle continued for centuries. Indeed the roof and towers of the present castle date back to the 1720s. In 1837 the castle was converted into a prison. A women's ward was created in 1881 and all the women prisoners in Finland were transferred there. The last inmates occupied cells as recently as 1993. The castle is now a museum and visitors can inspect the old cells which have been kept just as they were when the last prisoners left. Managed by the Finnish National Museum, the restored castle has various facilities for arranging exhibitions and meetings and there is also a cafeteria for visitors.

In Hattula, not far from Hämeenlinna Castle, is the beautiful Church of the Holy Cross. Together with the castle, this church is one of the oldest brick buildings in Finland and provides a rare glimpse into a stage of the country's cultural heritage. Work on the church was started in the fourteenth century. The murals were painted towards the end of the Catholic era in Finland between 1510 and 1522. There are some 180 paintings covering themes from the Creation to the Last Judgement. Other murals depict events in the lives of Mary and Jesus. The artists, whose names have not been preserved, were all Finns.

HEUREKA - A SCIENCE CENTRE FOR EVERYONE

Designed by Mikko Heikkinen and Markku Komonen – two of Finland's best known contemporary architects – and completed in 1989, Heureka is a unique, ultra-modern building which houses Finland's leading scientific activity centre. The centre provides an introduction to the achievements of modern science and is suitable for visitors of all ages. Besides a wide range of permanent displays, Heureka hosts several major international special exhibitions on history and science. The building also houses the Verne Theatre, a 500m^2 hemispheric auditorium, which gives the audience an extraordinary three-dimensional experience.

The front entrance of the Heureka Science Centre features a wide selection of geological samples from all over Finland. Its flowering plants are classified according to a system which was devised by the Swedish naturalist Carl von Linné (1707–1778) and continues to be as serviceable today as it was during his lifetime.

The Heureka Science Centre is popular with visitors of all ages. The centre collaborates with similar centres abroad. Themed exhibitions arranged at Heureka often attract hundreds of thousands of visitors.

The White Capital of the North

Visitors travelling on tram 3T on a circular line through Helsinki are provided with information about the sights along the way. In the background is the central railway station which was designed by Eliel Saarinen.

The city of Helsinki was founded in 1550 at the mouth of the River Vantaa by King Gustavus Vasa of Sweden. The river's waters pass through the Helsinki rapids just before they reach the sea and this geographical feature gave the city its modern Swedish name. Helsinki did not expand at first and it was not until Queen Christina had the city moved to its present site in 1640 that it began to achieve greater prominence.

Helsinki really began to flourish in 1748 when construction work began on the Suomenlinna Fortress. The purpose of this stronghold was to serve as a naval and military base to repel any attack by the Russians. The Swedish Parliament commissioned Augustin Ehrensvärd, an officer in the armed forces and one of the leading experts of his day in fortification technology, to design the island fortress of Sveaborg. This, it was hoped, would defend Finland against the growing threat from St. Petersburg.

At first Ehrensvärd encountered some difficulties. There were only 1,500 people living in Helsinki at the time and there was a severe shortage of materials, tools and workers for the construction project. The island itself was home to only a handful of fishermen and their families. Consequently, Ehrensvärd was assigned a couple of thousand infantrymen to work on the foundations of the fortress.

Before his death at his official residence near Turku in 1772, Ehrensvärd had been rewarded for his work by King Gustav III and elevated to the rank of field-marshal. Saddened by the demise of his old friend, the king himself designed Ehrensvärd's tomb. However, it was not until 1807 that the tomb was erected at the behest of King Gustav IV Adolf. It now stands in a small park in the middle of the great castle courtyard at Suomenlinna.

The very next year the fortress finally fell into the hands of Ehrensvärd's sworn enemies, the Russians.

Suomenlinna is now one of Helsinki's most popular tourist attractions. Its wealth of museums, fortifications, exhibitions, special events, beaches, restaurants and cafés can keep visitors occupied for hours on end. The best place to start exploring is probably the tour guide centre in the middle of the island complex. Visitors arriving in Helsinki by car ferry also get a spectacular initial view of the fortress as the ferry plies the narrow Kustaanmiekka sound, just a few yards from the fortified cliffs of the old stronghold.

Helsinki Market Square adjoins the South Harbour which serves as the departure point for several summer sight-seeing cruises to the offshore archipelago. The Market Square is one of the most popular spots in the city whatever the time of year. The atmosphere is unique, with fishmongers trading at the waterside and seagulls

On May Day the statue of Havis Amanda is traditionally crowned with a student cap by students of the Helsinki University of Technology. The statue is a popular meeting place. When Ville Vallgren's sculpture was unveiled in 1908 its nudity was severely criticised.

Guidebooks for tourists are available in several languages.

The Market Square in Helsinki has been nominated several times for the title of best market place in the world.

circling overhead in the hope that some tasty morsel will come their way. Semi-tame mallard ducks strut along the waterline with similar motives. On the western side of the Market Square, at the end of the Esplanade, stands the charming statue of Havis Amanda by the sculptor Ville Vallgren. This naked young girl in a fountain was a source of great controversy when the statue was unveiled in 1908.

A short walk along one of the narrow streets to the north of the Market Square leads the visitor to the Senate Square, the administrative and cultural heart of the city. In 1811 Emperor Alexander I ordered the complete renovation of Helsinki. The city was due to become the nation's capital in the following year and consequently two highly esteemed men were appointed to plan the renovation of the city. Between 1812 and 1825 the Swede Johan Albrekt Ehrenström drew up a new city plan for Helsinki and in 1816 the German-born Finnish architect Carl Ludwig Engel designed the imposing city centre buildings, which continue to dominate the architecture of the area to this very day. The Senate Square is steeped in history. A statue of Emperor Alexander II from 1894 by the sculptor Walter Runeberg stands in the middle of the square.

Engel also designed the first public monument to be erected in Helsinki. The Empress Stone stands in the middle of the Market Square and is dedicated to the memory of Alexandra, the wife of Emperor Nicholas I, who donated a large sum of money to the poor during her visit to Helsinki. The monument was erected by the city's wealthier citizens as a mark of gratitude to the empress.

The area around the central railway station is the modern commercial centre of Helsinki. Adjacent to the station, the main post office building houses the excellent Postal Museum – a place of pilgrimage for all serious stamp collectors. Established in 1926, the museum now gives visitors an opportunity to use state-of-the-art technology to explore the history of postal services both in Finland – where official postal services began in 1636 – and in other countries. The museum shop also sells first day covers and other philatelic treasures.

Finland's national gallery, the Ateneum, is the most highly regarded art institution in the country. It is also located near the central railway station and the building itself, designed by the architect Theodor Höijer, dates from 1887. In those days many artists sought to encourage a spirit of Finnish nationhood – an aspiration embodied in the words of Patria (the fatherland) which appear on the wall of the Ateneum building.

Besides various permanent collections and many visiting exhibitions, the building also serves as a venue for a wide range of cultural events.

Exhibitions of contemporary art from Finland and abroad are now housed in the Kiasma Museum of Contemporary Art, opened in 1998.

The most popular tourist attraction in Helsinki is the Rock Church in Temppeliaukio. Hewn out of solid rock

The Suomenlinna fortress in the background can also be reached in the winter on an ice-breaking ferryboat.

and illuminated through the roof, the building bears little resemblance to a conventional church when viewed from the outside. It was designed by two brothers, Timo and Tuomo Suomalainen, and was completed in 1969. Natural stone was used to construct the church and its ceiling is shrouded in copper. The walls are brought to life by running water which enters through fissures in the stone and flows out through channels under the floor. The church is a popular concert venue due to its excellent acoustics.

The Finns are a nation of sport-lovers. The country has produced several world-class ski jumpers, while Finland's racing and rally drivers have achieved international fame and won many world championships in recent years. The man voted the finest athlete of all time – the runner Paavo Nurmi – was also a Finn. His famous statue stands outside the Helsinki Olympic Stadium and has been photographed countless times by sport-lovers from all over the world.

The Swimming Stadium next to the Olympic Stadium is a welcome oasis in the summertime. The water is warm, even in cooler weather, so the facility remains open to the public from spring until autumn.

The Finnish National Museum was designed by the same three architects who designed the villa in Hvitträsk: Gesellius, Lindgren and Saarinen. The museum was completed in 1912.

The vaulted chambers of Suomenlinna have many stories to tell about Finland's history. In the summertime children can take part in guided adventure tours inside the chambers.

Korkeasaari Zoo, where you can see real bears, can also be reached by boat.

The Orthodox Uspensky Cathedral.

КО МНѢ ВСИ ТРУЖДАЮЩИСѦ И
БРЕМЕНЕННИИ И АЗЪ УПОКОЮ

Temppeliaukio Church is one of the most beautiful modern church buildings in Finland.

The Finlandia Concert Hall was designed by the architect Alvar Aalto in 1971. It has served as the venue for many international conferences and concerts are held there on a regular basis.

The Helsinki Olympic Games held in 1952 were characterised by the spirit of good sportsmanship.

The Kiasma Museum of Contemporary Art was designed by the American architect Stephen Holl.

KIASMA

From the Market Square you can take a red 'pub tram' which clatters around the city.

Here you can feel the spirit of Helsinki

When the Suomenlinna fortress fell and Helsinki capitulated to the Russians in 1808, Finland became an autonomous grand duchy under Russian rule. In 1811 Emperor Alexander I ordered the complete renovation of Helsinki and in 1812 the small town with just 5,000 inhabitants became the new capital. At the behest of the Emperor, the architects Ehrenström and Engels designed the Senate Square where a statue of Alexander II stands in front of Helsinki Cathedral. Today Helsinki has a population of half a million.

THE ORTHODOX CHURCH IN FINLAND

The walls of the Orthodox church in Iisalmi were painted by the Russian artists Loupanov and Feodorov who completed the frescoes in 1995.

The oldest and most atmospheric Orthodox church building in Helsinki, the Church of the Holy Trinity, was designed by C.L. Engel in 1827. This small church is close by the Lutheran Cathedral. Not far away in Katajanokka, overlooking the Market Square and South Harbour, stands the imposing Uspensky Cathedral constructed in 1868. This building, with its golden domes, was designed by the Russian architect Gornostayev. The name Uspensky, by which the cathedral is popularly known, is derived from the Russian word *uspenie* meaning ascension. The Orthodox faith has some 50,000 followers in Finland.

The Orthodox Church Museum in Kuopio was established in 1957. The area had been ceded to the Soviet Union after the end of World War II and the aim was to continue the museum work begun in 1911 at the Orthodox monastery on the island of Valamo on Lake Ladoga. Some of the artefacts on display also come from the former Finnish monastery at Konevitsa which now also lies on the Russian side of the border. Items were also brought here from the Pechenga region in the far north which suffered a similar fate. The objective was to salvage the Finnish Orthodox heritage from the war and from shifting international borders, although a great deal had to be left behind.

The Valamo Monastery was originally established by the monk Sergei on an island on the great Lake Ladoga at the end of the fourteenth century. After it had been rebuilt in 1715 by Emperor Peter the Great following a serious fire, the monastery, with its two thousand monks, became an important centre for Orthodoxy in the region. The Orthodox Church Museum in Kuopio provides a unique opportunity to examine monastic treasures and to explore the significance of the monasteries as places of pilgrimage.

Valamo Monastery at Heinävesi is a living centre of Orthodox culture and religion.

The monks of Valamo Monastery had to leave their home in 1939 and join in the evacuation of the Finnish Karelian population to the west. They found a new home at Heinävesi in 1940. The elderly monks were few in number and this made life in their new surroundings difficult. Since the 1970s, however, there has been a revival of the Orthodox monastic life and nowadays New Valamo, the home of the Finnish Orthodox monks, has become a very popular destination for visitors. The monastery even has its own hotel to accommodate many of its guests.

A short scenic journey from the monastery brings visitors to the Lintula Convent. This convent was also formerly on the Karelian Isthmus where it was founded in 1895. However, like the Valamo monks, the nuns of Lintula were evacuated to Finland during the war. They now make their living making wax candles.

The evacuee centre at Iisalmi, with its small domed church, is one of the prettiest spots in the North Savo region. It serves as a Karelian-Orthodox cultural centre, seeking to revive the old culture on the Finnish side of the new international border and features an exhibition of scale models of some seventy churches and Orthodox chapels which remained on the Russian side of the border.

The interior of the modest domed church, which is dedicated to the prophet Elijah, comes as a surprise to its visitors. The walls and interior of the dome were painted by the Russian artists Loupanov and Feodorov. The frescoes, which were painted by them in the twelfth to fourteenth-century Slavic style, are stunningly beautiful. The walls of the assembly hall in the evacuee centre were painted by the Greek frescoist Andonopoulos in the ancient Byzantine style of thousands of years ago. The beautiful stained glass windows in the great hall were created in the nineteenth-century tradition by the Russian artist Nikitenko.

In the summer *tsasounas* serve as centres of Orthodox *praasniekka* village festivals on the commemorative days of their respective patron saints.

The term *tsasouna* is used to describe a Karelian Orthodox chapel or small prayer house. These are usually wooden buildings with icons on the back wall and they include an icon to the saint to whom the *tsasouna* is dedicated. The only old *tsasouna* remaining in Finland after World War II was built in 1790 at Hattuvaara in the Ilomantsi district of North Karelia. In the summertime the *tsasounas* and small Orthodox churches of contemporary Finnish Karelia serve as centres for the *praasniekka*

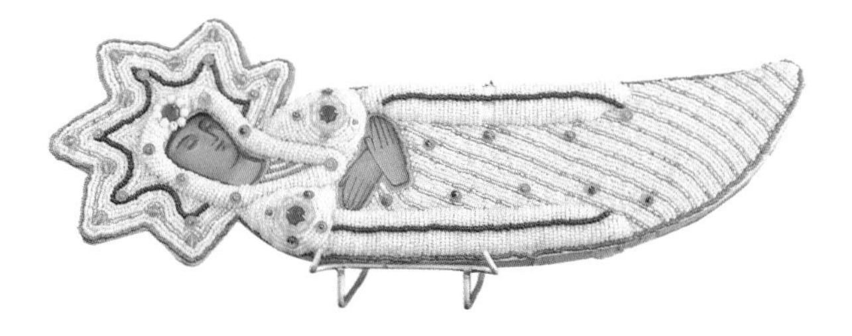

The burial icon of the Mother of God is a priceless relic brought from the Konevitsa monastery to the Orthodox Church Museum in Kuopio.

A Village Straight Out of The Kalevala Epic Poem

North and South Karelia have always been midway between the east and west and so it is here that quarrel-mongers from these hemispheres have always fought and settled their differences. These territories have changed hands several times, going first to one side and then the other, as a result of various peace treaties. Through all of this, however, the Karelian population has remained fundamentally Karelian in character and sentiment to this day, even though the standard of living of eastern Karelians nowadays is much lower than that of their western counterparts. The municipality of Ilomantsi in North Karelia has become better known in recent years as the easternmost point of the European Union. Even before this, however, the area was well-known to the Finns because North Karelia was the place where the 26-year-old physician Elias Lönnrot made his very first journey in 1828 to collect poetry and songs which later became the Finnish national epic poem, the Kalevala. In Kesälahti Lönnrot met Juhana Kainulainen, a local bard, whom he asked to sing traditional songs under the shade of a great pine tree. Kainulainen knew a great many incantations which he sang to the gods of the forest to ensure good luck on hunting expeditions and Lönnrot pains-takingly transcribed

Orthodox homes have a devotional corner with an icon, a sacred image painted on wood. Around the icon is a cloth embroidered by one of the women in the household.

these songs from dawn to dusk.

The result of the journeys made by Lönnrot and others who followed his example were the original Kalevala collection (1835–1836), the Kanteletar collection (1840–1841) and the new Kalevala (1849). This last collection is the one we know and use today and has been translated into nearly fifty languages.

The two hallmarks of the Karelian area are poetry and handicrafts. The songs of the region tell of life and death, hopes and dreams, joys and sorrows. The image of the Karelian soul bird, which brought news from a greater unknown world, was embroidered on a cloth kept in a special place by the door, next to the wash basin or around the icons in a devotional corner. These textiles, on which women of old sewed their innermost secrets, are now on display at the Ilomantsi handicrafts centre and in the museums of North Karelia.

The Orthodox church of St. Elijah and a Lutheran church, which is beautifully decorated with one hundred and sixteen angels, stand side by side in Ilomantsi. Visitors can explore the traditional Karelian culture and way of life at the bard's farmhouse in the rune singers' village. There are also regular opportunities to enjoy the Finnish music of old performed on the original folk instrument, the kantele, as well as to hear recitations of Kalevala poetry.

Fine food and wine are an integral part of the Orthodox faith and the rune singers' village offers all the delicacies of Karelian cuisine. Tourists can also visit the wine tower at the local Pelto-Hermann vineyard in Pappilanvaara. The walls of the lift, which provides access to the former water tower, are decorated with amusing paintings illustrating the wisdom of experience. From the top of the tower there are some spectacular views over the broad and scenic countryside of Ilomantsi with its lakes and hills.

The stories of the Kalevala evolved over the course of several centuries in the gloom of the Finnish forests. The physician, writer and collector of folklore Elias Lönnrot collected these old stories and poems which were first published in 1836. A new, extended edition was published in 1849. The Kalevala was an important work in the development of Finnish national consciousness.

Ruunaa – The Rapids and Their Beautiful Natural Surroundings

Surrounding a chain of rapids in the eastern part of the Finnish North Karelian town of Lieksa lies the camping and recreation centre of Ruunaa. The River Lieksa was formerly an important log driving passage until log driving ceased in 1984. The timber structures used for driving have, however, been preserved to enable future generations to study them. The best way to explore the rapids of Ruunaa is to shoot them in a whitewater boat steered by an experienced helmsman. The longest shooting distance is some thirty kilometres. There are still five wild rapids and, while they look magnificent and dangerous, it is possible to shoot them quite safely in a good strong whitewater boat, provided life jackets and safety helmets are worn. When the last of the rapids has been negotiated successfully, a delicious meal in a tranquil pastoral setting awaits the intrepid traveller. The Ruunaa area is also a real paradise for those who enjoy fishing.

The town of Lieksa is situated on the banks of the beautiful Lake Pielinen. Opposite the town are the rugged tree-covered hills of Koli National Park. In the Pielinen outdoor museum, which is located in the border area with Russia, you can discover where eastern and western civilisations meet.

The rapids at the magnificent recreational area in Ruunaa can be explored either by shooting the rapids in a whitewater boat or by following the marked trails along the banks of the river. The longest shooting distance through the rapids is 30 kilometres.

Kainuu – A Friendly County

Kainuu is one of Finland's poorest areas. Life there has always been hard due to depression and crop failures which ravaged the district for centuries. In those difficult times people were forced to eat bark bread – rye bread baked with a mixture of rye flour and finely-ground bark of a pine tree. Modern health enthusiasts have discovered the nutritious properties of bark bread and claim that it provides people with the much-needed fibre often lacking in today's diet!

Tar burning came to the rescue of the district's economy in the 1800s. Tar was burned and then transported in large tar boats along the huge Lake Oulu to the town of Oulu, where it was sold to local tar merchants or sometimes exchanged for rye flour. This was Kainuu's main livelihood, albeit very labour intensive and often the result of blood, sweat and tears. The process of turning pine trees into tar could take as long as three years. When tar ceased to be in demand Kainuu's economy suffered another crash. This state of affairs lasted until the onset of the rebuilding programme in the neighbouring Russian town of Kostamus. Work was provided for local men and Kainuu's economy underwent a temporary resurgence as a result. Nowadays, because of the depression in the Russian economy, the people of Kainuu send food and clothing to Kostamus, not the other way around. Kainuu shares a 260-kilometre stretch of border with Russia. On the other side of the border lies magnificient scenery and nature in all its glory. Here Kainuu's travel companies arrange safe fishing, hunting and cultural visits.

The Kainuu are among the most hospitable and friendly people in Finland and the entire area of Kainuu is one of the country's most beautiful districts. The Kuhmo Chamber Music Festival has evolved from humble beginnings to a major annual event, making Kuhmo famous around the world in the process. Kuhmo is also the location of the excellent Kalevala village where visitors can learn about the characters and locations of Finland's national epic poem, Kalevala. Marked nature trails of varying lengths are available to those who wish to explore the tranquillity of the great wilderness. Although it is not an especially affluent region, in addition to its many sites, Kainuu is able to offer visitors some delicious local produce. Nowhere in Finland can you sample tastier fish dishes. These dishes are prepared in a variety of ways from fish freshly caught in one of Kainuu's lakes.

The Wildest Part of Finland

You can catch brown trout in the rivers and lakes of Kuusamo.

Kuusamo is a paradise for nature-loving visitors. It is the land of bare mountains and deep rivers running through magnificent ravines. It is also the land of great rapids. The famous rapids of the River Kitka run wild and free. Some of the rapids are so awesome that it is advisable to listen to their surge and enjoy them from the safety of dry land. The description of national parks earlier in the book mentioned Oulanka National Park which is one of Finland's most popular parks.

Oulanka is one of Kuusamo's key nature attractions. The centre of the area's winter tourism is Ruka mountain which is also the base for the majority of local tour operators all year round.

The best way to cross a swamp is using duckboards.

A tributary of the Oulankajoki River, the Kitkajoki River in Oulanka National Park twists and turns for over 35 kilometres.

A solitary fisherman swathed in the mist raised by the sun's warmth.

The wild rapids in Kuusamo can be shot safely with an experienced helmsman steering the boat.

Peaceful nature in Kuusamo
Located on the border between Lapland and the rest of Finland, Kuusamo has many bare mountains and deep rivers running through ravines. In Oulanka National Park the rivers run through mighty rapids but the landscape also has its quiet spots which you will remember long after you've returned home. They are like works of art painted by nature and it's invigorating just to look at them.
The busy tourist centre with its many facilities is situated at the foot of the Rukatunturi mountain.

The winter months are not dark
In Lapland the sun sinks below the horizon in mid-December and does not rise again until mid-January. This time of year is called *kaamos* but, contrary to what one might expect, it is not dark and the sky is filled with shades ranging from pale blue to pale violet. Lapland's very own bird is the Siberian jay, *Perisoreus infaustus.* The bird is friendly by nature and likes to accompany tourists on their travels.

Lapland

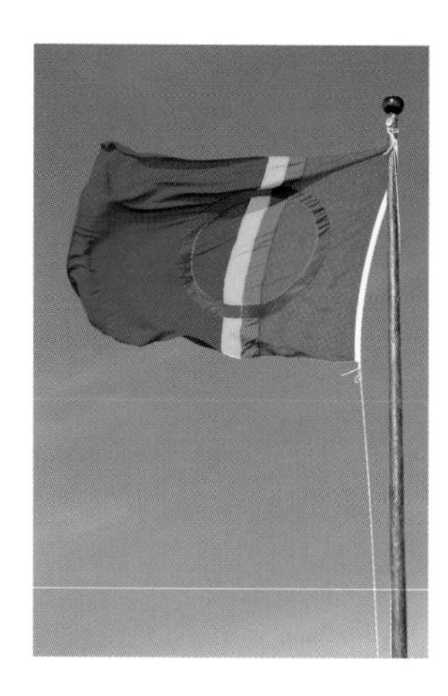

The history of Lapland describes how man first ventured into this inhospitable wilderness, used it as a hunting ground, gradually learned how to till the land and later established small hamlets in areas formerly ruled by the forces of nature.

Nobody knows exactly how long Lapland has been inhabited. Ten thousand years ago there were people living on the shores of the Atlantic and the Arctic Oceans, as well as on the banks of the rivers that flow into the northern parts of the Gulf of Bothnia. We do not know for certain to which race these people belonged or what language they spoke. We only know that the southern tribes robbed those ancient inhabitants of their lands and that Finns or Vikings later forced the Sami tribe ever further north. Based on rock drawings and artefacts excavated from graves, we can safely say that these parts have been inhabited since the end of the Ice Age.

The entire north, or *Ultima Thule* as the Roman historian Tacitus first described it, was for a long time a hunting ground for both the eastern and the western tribes. Lapps, or the Sami people, were pushed even further north as the forests and salmon-filled rivers were plundered by the newcomers. The southern culture spread slowly towards the retreating north. World War II brought great unrest for Lapland, with the northern regions of both Finland and Norway being turned into battlegrounds and facing massive destruction. In Finland, for instance, there is only one village, Suvanto, where one can see complete examples of traditional Sami architecture. The other villages and communities were more or less razed to the ground by the retreating Germans in the final stages of warfare.

There are ten different dialects of the Sami language. The Finnish Sami speak three of them: Northern Sami, Inari and Koltta. The Kolttas are Orthodox Christians. A few of them live in Finland and a few more live along the Russian border in Norway, while the remainder live in the border regions of Russia.

Sami music, called *joik*, contains very few words and has neither a beginning nor an end. The Sami people see *joik* as a way of commemorating others. Many Sami people are very accomplished artists, singers and writers.

Reindeer rallies are held throughout Lapland.

The Sami wear their colourful traditional costume on weekdays too.
The lasso carried over the shoulder is for catching runaway reindeer.

Rounding up reindeer is a test of strength.

The Lapp tent, called a *kota*, has a hole in the roof to allow smoke to escape from the fire in the middle of the tent.

Aurora Borealis

Among Lapland's most beautiful natural spectacles is the *Aurora Borealis*, also known as the Northern Lights. These days many Lapp hotels employ a night watchman to knock on the doors of foreign guests when this rare phenomenon occurs. His call is eloquent: "Quickly everyone, the heavenly bonfires are lit and are burning brightly!" During the winter months the Arctic regions are ruled by a blue-grey, eerily quiet polar night. This is the time when the frosty northern sky presents various shades of green, white and red and daintily dancing spectacles of light that dart up and down and from side to side. Old Sami folk believe that the *Aurora Borealis* is created when a fox brushes the snow drifts with its bushy tail, sending particles of snow into the air to create lights in different colours. Sadly there is no truth to this wonderful legend. The magnificent light spectacles take place at an altitude of one hundred kilometres and are linked with magnetic storms and sunspots. The *Aurora Borealis* is the result of an earth-bound electromagnetic shower of particles (solar flux).

Gold in Lapland

Finland's largest national park in Lemmenjoki is also famous for its mighty rivers, the most famous of which is the 70-kilometre long Lemmenjoki River. It is surrounded by mountains which are 500 metres high. Lemmenjoki is an excellent location for the discriminating and experienced hiker and the area's main attraction is its valley.

In Kultala, by the Morgamojoki River, there is an information point dealing with gold prospecting in Lapland. Gold has been found in several places in Lapland and the region has been the focus of two gold rushes. Ivalo and Lemmenjoki are the most famous prospecting rivers.

In Tankavaara, south of Ivalo, visitors can try their luck at panning for gold. Tankavaara is also home to the Gold Museum which describes gold prospecting past and present. Professional gold prospectors began to show amateurs how to use a gold pan in the 1970s. They probably decided that the money brought in by tourists provided a more reliable income than the nuggets they could find. Annual gold prospecting championships are also held in Tankavaara.

The pipe is ever-present when a Lapp shaman meditates on the mysteries of nature.

The Siida Sami Museum

In Inari, in northern Lapland, there is a Sami museum called Siida, which acquired a fine new building in 1998. It was designed by the architect Juhani Pallasmaa. The museum complex also includes some ancient buildings that formerly belonged to the old Inari museum which, along with a collection of historical objects, tell us about the history and life of the Sami people.

Part of the museum introduces us to Sami domestic industry which has played an important part in Sami families' daily lives for hundreds of years. Old Sami objects were always made for some practical purpose and nothing was ever wasted. For instance, every single part of a slaughtered reindeer was used. Genuine Sami handicrafts are sold under the name Sami Duodji. Objects are made of reindeer bones, skin and wood. The large wooden Lapp ladle, known as a *kuksa*, is a skilfully hand-made work of art fashioned from willow or birch. It is commonly used at campfires to serve freshly brewed coffee. The colours of the *Aurora Borealis* feature prominently on Lapp textiles.

The new Siida Museum also contains displays about Sami culture and natural phenomena. In addition, it houses the Forest and Park Service's nature centre, which provides visitors with information about Lapland and its ecology. Sami culture has always revolved around the annual cycle of nature. The museum is situated in a beautiful location on the banks of a vast lake. According to Sami belief, thunder was always worshipped before other gods. The locals call thunder *Ukko* and this translates loosely as 'old man'. One of the most important sites for *Ukko* worship is an island called Ukonsaari which lies at the westernmost end of Lake Inari. Sacrificial horns were found on this island as late as 1910. The Reformation destroyed many of the artefacts connected with Sami beliefs and culture, including beautiful and skilfully-manufactured witch drums. Clergymen such as Tuderus, who lived in the 1640s, deemed their own beliefs the only correct ones and consequently smashed and burned a great many of these drums. The only witch drums spared during the purges can now be found in the museums of Leipzig, Stockholm and Copenhagen. Fortunately modern artisans are able to reproduce them as souvenirs for tourists.

You can still find genuine Sami craftwork made from natural materials in Inari.

THE KEMI SNOW CASTLE

The world's greatest snow castle was first built in Kemi at the mouth of the Gulf of Bothnia in 1996. Its fame spread instantly and it has since become an annual event. The huge snow castle hosts concerts, live theatre, weddings and religious services. The construction of the castle always starts at the beginning of the year, depending on the prevailing snow conditions. Once inside you can sit on a chair made of snow and enjoy a meal in the snow restaurant.

From January through to April visitors can test their stamina in Kemi in the restaurants, hotel suites or in the chapel of the world's biggest snow castle. Some people even go there to work out.

A real ice-breaker takes tourists on an excursion from Kemi Port to the ice-fields far out at sea.

Arktikum House

On the banks of the River Ounas in Rovaniemi, the capital of Lapland, stands a magnificent building where it is possible to learn why life in the dark, solitary, cold north is such a continuous challenge for those living in this inhospitable region. You can dive hundreds of metres into the depths of the northern Barents Sea or discover the secrets of the shamans. One large exhibition area in the museum contains a huge arctic zone which enables visitors to grasp the true size of Greenland, the biggest island in the world.

Arktikum is a window on the arctic world. Designed in 1992 by a group of Danish architects – Birch-Bonderup & Thorup-Waade – this magnificent building houses a museum that is divided in two: the Lapp provincial museum and the arctic centre of the University of Lapland.

From the end of November until the middle of January the sun never rises in Lapland. This period is referred to as polar night. Around Christmas time the polar night is at its most beautiful and the landscape is ablaze with varying shades of blue, lilac and pink. The whiteness of the snow and the starlit sky alone make the nights seem bright, not to mention the effects of the stunning *Aurora Borealis*.

During the summer, which lasts from May to July, the sun in northern Lapland never sets at all. It is daylight twenty-four hours a day.

A young skier acquaints himself with modern lapland and its ski slopes.

A young Sami boy guards the fire made by the men and watches over the coffee pot in which real Finnish *pannukahvi,* with its fine, unique taste, is being made.

Driving a reindeer sleigh is not easy at first because the animal immediately knows when it has a tourist on board and tries to overturn the sleigh. However, learning how to handle the reindeer is not difficult and you will end up with a real reindeer driving licence to take home with you.

Visitors can stay overnight in the wilderness huts in winter. If you're lucky, someone will have stayed there the night before.

Many tourist centres in Lapland offer rides in sleighs drawn by friendly huskies.

You may need some instruction before riding a snowmobile for the first time.

Lapland, with its many downhill ski slopes and cross-country skiing trails, is a favourite region for winter sports.

Santa at Home

The Finnish Santa Claus lives deep inside a mountain in his secret hideaway home in the border region of Korvatunturi. The mountain gets its name from the three 'ears' which Santa uses to listen to the wishes of children from all over the world. He has chosen this tranquil setting as his home so that nobody can surprise him, his wife and the hundreds of elves who toil away month after month preparing presents. However, Santa often visits various locations, such as the mountain hotels and the airport, where he welcomes planes bringing in foreign visitors. His headquarters are at Santa's Pajakylä (workshop village) north of Rovaniemi. Here Santa has his own wonderful post office where he meets people daily. You can even have your photo taken with Santa.

A new theme park called Santapark was opened in 1998. It is devoted to the myth of Santa Claus and is linked to Pajakylä by road. Near Santapark is Santa's own reindeer park where visitors can try riding the semi-domesticated authentic mode of transport of the indigenous Sami population.

The Finnish Santa Claus lives in his secret hideaway home in the border region of Korvatunturi (Ear Mountain). Santa uses his three 'ears' to listen to the wishes of children from all over the world.

In December dozens of charter planes arrive at Rovaniemi, bringing Christmas visitors who want to find out about snow, reindeer and Santa. Of course, they also want to buy their Christmas presents in the shops of Pajakylä. A winter holiday in Lapland is a great experience. The many wonderful local mountain hotels have masses of snow and excitement to offer the winter visitor. Reindeer, snowmobiles and huskies are much more common modes of transport than cars in the Sami landscape.

Santa Park was opened near Rovaniemi in 1998. The park is equipped with the latest technology and outside there is a real reindeer park. Santa has his very own post office in nearby Pajakylä.

The winter months and the frost conspire to fashion trees into exquisite works of art.

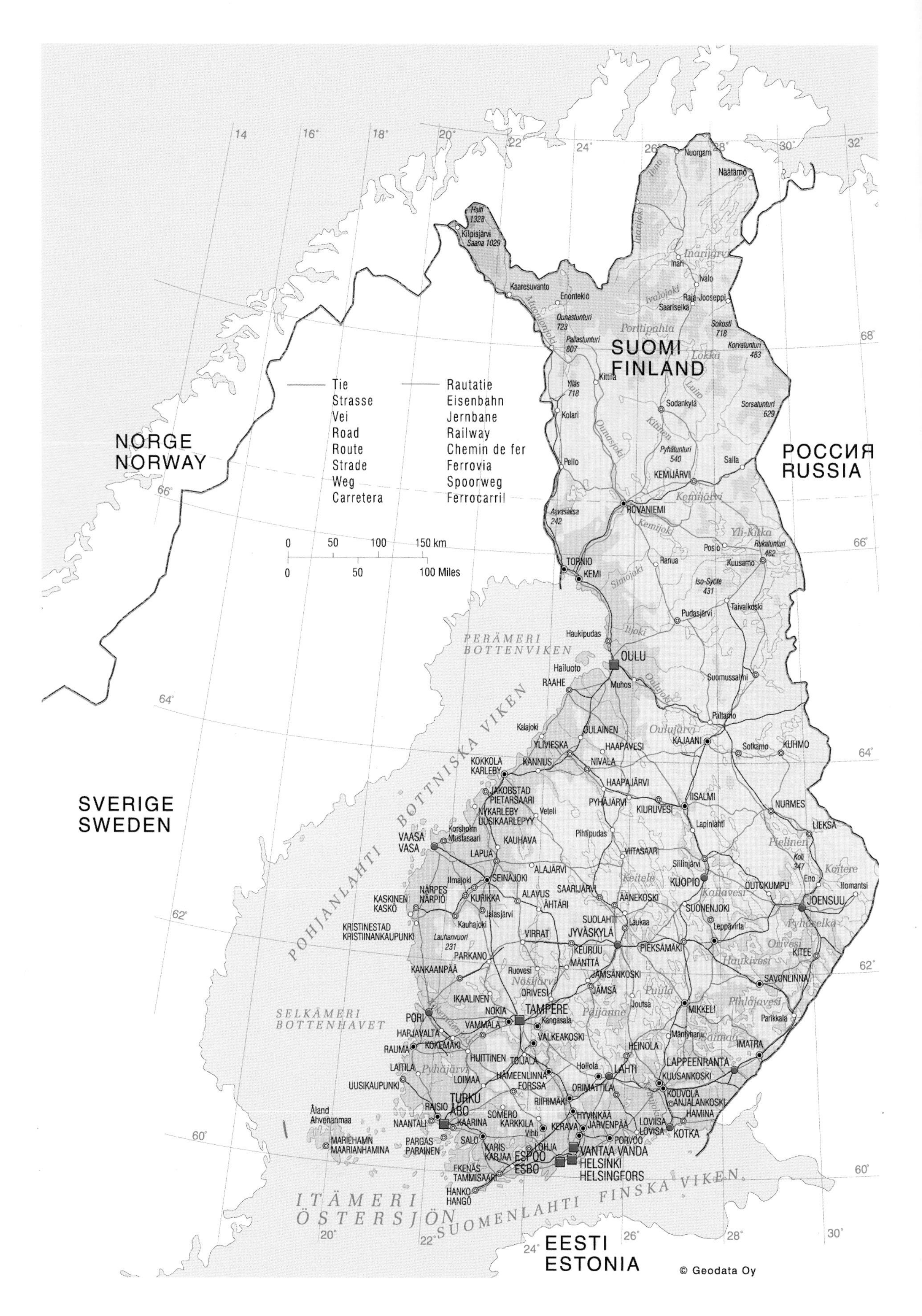

SUOMI
FINLAND
NORGE
NORWAY
SVERIGE
SWEDEN
РОССИЯ
RUSSIA
EESTI
ESTONIA
Tie
Strasse
Vei
Road
Route
Strade
Weg
Carretera
Rautatie
Eisenbahn
Jernbane
Railway
Chemin de fer
Ferrovia
Spoorweg
Ferrocarril
0 50 100 150 km
0 50 100 Miles
PERÄMERI
BOTTENVIKEN
POHJANLAHTI BOTTNISKA VIKEN
SELKÄMERI
BOTTENHAVET
ITÄMERI
ÖSTERSJÖN
SUOMENLAHTI FINSKA VIKEN
Nuorgam
Näätämö
Halti 1328
Kilpisjärvi
Saana 1029
Inarijärvi
Inari
Ivalo
Raja-Jooseppi
Saariselkä
Kaaresuvanto
Enontekiö
Ounastunturi 723
Pallastunturi 807
Porttipahta
Sokosti 718
Korvatunturi 483
Lokka
Kittilä
Ylläs 718
Kolari
Sodankylä
Sorsatunturi 629
Pyhätunturi 540
Pello
Salla
KEMIJÄRVI
ROVANIEMI
Aavasaksa 242
Posio
Rukatunturi 462
Kuusamo
TORNIO
KEMI
Ranua
Iso-Syöte 431
Pudasjärvi
Taivalkoski
Haukipudas
OULU
Hailuoto
RAAHE
Muhos
Suomussalmi
Paltamo
Kalajoki
OULAINEN
Oulujärvi
KAJAANI
YLIVIESKA
HAAPAVESI
Sotkamo
KUHMO
KOKKOLA
KARLEBY
KANNUS
NIVALA
HAAPAJÄRVI
JAKOBSTAD
PIETARSAARI
PYHÄJÄRVI
KIURUVESI
IISALMI
NURMES
NYKARLEBY
UUSIKAARLEPYY
Veteli
Lapinlahti
LIEKSA
VAASA
VASA
Korsholm
Mustasaari
KAUHAVA
Pihtipudas
Pielinen
Koli 347
VIITASAARI
LAPUA
Siilinjärvi
Koitere
ALAJÄRVI
Ilmajoki
SEINÄJOKI
KUOPIO
OUTOKUMPU
Eno
Ilomantsi
SAARIJÄRVI
NÄRPES
NÄRPIÖ
KURIKKA
ALAVUS
ÄÄNEKOSKI
KASKINEN
KASKÖ
ÄHTÄRI
JOENSUU
SUONENJOKI
Jalasjärvi
SUOLAHTI
KRISTINESTAD
KRISTIINANKAUPUNKI
Kauhajoki
Laukaa
Leppävirta
Pyhäselkä
Lauhanvuori 231
VIRRAT
JYVÄSKYLÄ
PIEKSÄMÄKI
Orivesi
KITEE
PARKANO
KEURUU
MÄNTTÄ
Haukivesi
KANKAANPÄÄ
Ruovesi
JÄMSÄNKOSKI
Puula
SAVONLINNA
Näsijärvi
ORIVESI
JÄMSÄ
IKAALINEN
Joutsa
Pihlajavesi
PORI
NOKIA
TAMPERE
Kangasala
Päijänne
MIKKELI
Parikkala
HARJAVALTA
VAMMALA
VALKEAKOSKI
Mäntyharju
Saimaa
RAUMA
KOKEMÄKI
HEINOLA
IMATRA
HUITTINEN
TOIJALA
LAPPEENRANTA
LAITILA
Pyhäjärvi
HÄMEENLINNA
Hollola
LAHTI
UUSIKAUPUNKI
LOIMAA
FORSSA
ORIMATTILA
KUUSANKOSKI
RAISIO
TURKU
ÅBO
RIIHIMÄKI
KOUVOLA
ANJALANKOSKI
Åland
Ahvenanmaa
NAANTALI
SOMERO
HYVINKÄÄ
HAMINA
KAARINA
KARKKILA
JÄRVENPÄÄ
LOVIISA
LOVISA
KOTKA
Vihti
KERAVA
MARIEHAMN
MAARIANHAMINA
PARGAS
PARAINEN
SALO
KARIS
KARJAA
LOHJA
PORVOO
ESPOO
ESBO
VANTAA VANDA
HELSINKI
HELSINGFORS
EKENÄS
TAMMISAARI
HANKO
HANGÖ
© Geodata Oy

© N.W. Damm & Søn AS
N-0055 Oslo
Tel.: +47 24 05 10 00
Fax: +47 24 05 12 92
E-mail: trude.lie@damm.no

Author: Sinikka Salokorpi
Design: Grafisk Design — Unni Dahl, Kristiansund.
Art Director: Bård Løken
Translation: Berlitz as
Repro: Larvik Litho as
Printed by: Narayana Press, Denmark

Distributed in Finland by:
Egmont Kustannus Oy Ab / KIRJALITO
Mikonkatu 13 A, 00100 Helsinki
Tel.: +358 201 332 222
Fax: +358 201 332 360

Printed in Denmark 2004

Picture credits:
Top = A
Top left = B
Top right = C
Bottom = D
Bottom left = E
Bottom right = F
Centre left = G
Centre right = H
Centre = I

Hannu Hautala: 1, 35D, 36A, 36D, 38D, 41B, 41D, 42-43,92B, 92D, 94, 95A, 96, 97C, 97F, 102, 111

Gorilla;
101C
Matti Niemi: 14G, 24A, 74D, 80F
Kari Autero: 32B
Henry Edman: 47D, 65D
Petri Kuokka: 75, 31I
Erkki Laine: 77
Aimo Hyvärinen: 80E
Timo Kilpeläinen: 90A
Harri Nurminen: 101H
Esko Männikkö: 108C
Renja Leino: 31A
Rippe Koskinen: 44D

Gorilla/Samfoto;
Ari Jaskari: 32G
Pirila Marja: 32F
Esko Männikkö: 33C
Jaakko Heikkilä: 33G
Henry Edman: 33E
Matti Niemi: 74A, 76,

Kuvasuomi Ky. Matti Kohlo:
11A,14F, 18, 19G, 19, 27, 26A, 28C, 28D, 28B, 29A, 41C, 46A, 52A, 52D, 53, 54A, 55, 59, 64, 67D, 68D, 70, 73, 81, 86, 87G, 87A, 88A, 103, 104, 105, 106A, 106D, 107A, 107D, 108E, 108F, 109, 110A, 110D

Studio Helsinki;
P. Harastel: 15

Mira/Samfoto;
Kalvero Ojutkangas: 2-3, 37, 100
Kent Klich: 29I

Mira;
Håkan Pieniowski: 38C
Kuvapörssi: 4-5, 26D, 78A, 78F, 79, 83A, 83F

Comma Finland OY;
6-7, 29D, 47A, 54D, 92C, 93A, 93D
Keijo Penttinen: 8
Esko Jämsä: 20E, 24D, 84-85

Jörg Frobitzsch: 20-21

Luonnonkuva-Arkisto;
34D, 61D
Keijo Penttinen: 12C
Markku Tario: 14A, 16-17, 22-23, 35A, 45, 88-89, 90-91,
Tero Poukkanen: 34A
Lassi Rautianien: 40A
Reijo Juurinen: 60D
Heikki Nikki: 71
Kalvero Ojutkangas: 68D
Tuomo Wuori: 78E
Patrik Bertrand: 82, 30
Jarmo Manninen: 98D
Arto Hämäläinen: 31D
Jari Salonen: 44

Toplyviä-Mononen: 25

Samfoto;
Per-Anders Rosenkvist: 32H
Nina Korhonen/Mira: 32E, 33B, 33H, 33F
JB. Olsen/R. Sørensen: 95F
Mimsy Møller: 108B

Bård Løken: 13, 39D, 40D, 60C, 61C, 98A

Teijo Määtänen: 46I

Kainuun Sanomat: 46D

Hackman IIttala OY;
Valto Kokko: 57
Indav: 56

Jorma Peiponen: 58A, 60B, 87D, 9, 10

Martti Roininen: 58D

Matti Kivekäs: 62, 63, 65B, 65C

Värisuomi OY: 80A

Premium: 99

Turku Provincial Puhakka: 11D, 50-51

Sinikka Salokorpi:
12C, 18, 26H, 29H, 66, 67A
68A, 69D, 76, 78A, 83E, 88A

Also available:

DESTINATIONS COLLECTION

The Best of Norway
Languages:
English
German
French
Dutch
Portuguese
Chinese
Finnish
Norwegian
Italian
Spanish
Russian
Japanese
Korean

CLASSIC COLLECTION

Norway – incl. CD
Languages:
English
German
Spanish
Japanese
Norwegian
French
Italian
Russian

A Taste of Norway
Languages:
Norwegian
English
German
French

Th. Kittelsen: Trolls
Languages:
English
German
Spanish
Japanese
Norwegian
French
Italian
Dutch

HISTORY COLLECTION

The Vikings
Languages:
English
German
Italian
Spanish
Swedish
Icelandic
Norwegian
Japanese
French
Dutch
Danish
Russian

Viking Cookbook
Languages:
English
Spanish
Norwegian
German
French
Danish

CHILDREN'S COLLECTION

Magnus Viking
Languages:
Norwegian
German
French
English
Spanish
Danish
Swedish

Elgar
Languages:
Norwegian
German
French
English
Spanish
Swedish

The Little Troll
Languages:
Norwegian
German
Spanish
Japanese
Swedish
English
French
Italian
Dutch

VIDEO COLLECTION

The Best of Norway

Format:	*Languages:*
VHS/PAL	English
VHS/NTSC	American
VHS/PAL	Norwegian
VHS/PAL	German
VHS/NTSC	Japanese
VHS/PAL	Italian
VHS/SECAM	French
VHS/PAL	Spanish
VHS/NTSC	Spanish
VHS/PAL	Korean